TIGER WOMAN

[*Vaughan & Freeman.*

BETTY MAY— " THE TIGER WOMAN "

TIGER WOMAN

My Story

by

BETTY MAY

Duckworth Overlook

LONDON & NEW YORK

This edition published in the UK in 2014 by
Duckworth Overlook

LONDON
30 Calvin Street, London E1 6NW
T: 020 7490 7300
E: info@duckworth-publishers.co.uk
www.ducknet.co.uk
For bulk and special sales please contact
sales@duckworth-publishers.co.uk,
or write to us at the above address.

NEW YORK
141 Wooster Street
New York, NY 10012
www.overlookpress.com

First published by
Gerald Duckworth & Co. Ltd in 1929

© 1929 by Betty May

A catalogue record for this book is available
from the British Library

ISBN 978-0-7156-4855-1

Printed and bound in Great Britain

CONTENTS

5

CHAPTER V

DRUGS AND DIVORCE

CHAPTER VI

THE MYSTIC

CHAPTER VII

THE ABBEY

CHAPTER VIII

I GO TO AMERICA

LIST OF ILLUSTRATIONS

INTRODUCTION

I SUPPOSE that a good many of the people who read this book (if any do!) will have heard of me already. Some of them will actually know me and remember the things and the people I am going to speak of. They will recognize several of the individuals who are called only by their Christian names, or who are only described by their appearance or most marked characteristics. For these it may be interesting to recall the old times of before and during the war—now that everything is so altered—and the adventures that we used to have in those days. But there will be a great many people who will never have heard of me at all, and for them I want to explain a little of myself if possible, before I begin. I want this to be a frank history of my life. By this I mean that I want people to realize what I am really like. A lot of the stories I am going to tell are, I suppose, rather unpleasant home-truths about myself, but I am not ashamed of them. They are all part of me, and when you have read my story perhaps you will understand in some way how my character has been formed.

When I read through this book the thing that struck me most was what an exciting life I have had up to the present (you see I am not even middle-aged yet). But in spite of this it has not really felt so exciting while it has all been going on. Of course bits of it have been thrilling, I admit. But then for long periods nothing seemed to happen to speak of, and I had no money or was terribly bored or something like that, and things did not seem bright at all. I suppose everybody's life really feels much like that however exciting it is, and I should be grateful for the experiences that I have had. I have only written down events that I thought would interest everybody because I thought otherwise no one would want to read the book, and one thing I should like to make clear is that the things which are likely to interest everybody are not always the things that have interested me most. I have had all sorts of experiences which mean a lot to me but would not interest anyone else to hear about. I suppose every woman carries in her heart memories that mean more to her than all sorts of exciting stories she might be able to tell. It is certainly so with me, and if there are people who know me and read my story and wonder about why this person or that episode has not been mentioned, it is possible that they may find an explanation in what I have said above. On the other hand, it may just be I that have forgotten, for it has not always been easy to remember every incident in one's life.

First of all you must realize that I have never tried to be ordinary and to fit in with other people. I have not cared what the world thought about me, and as a result I am afraid what it thought has often not been very kind. I have had love affairs, some of which you will hear about and some of which you will not hear about. I have often lived only for pleasure and excitement, but you will see that I came to it by unexpected ways. Fate seems to have led me there, for I have lived in a world which I was certainly not born to. In fact nothing could have been further from it than the surroundings in which I was brought up. And now having said this, I hope everyone will feel in a sympathetic mood to hear about me. If they do not they had better put my book down, for I am going to tell my story in the same sort of way that I have lived my life.

CHAPTER I

CHILDHOOD

Myself—Earliest memories—My coster grandmother—A suicide—I am sent to live with my father—My father's had character—His arrest by my grandfather—Life on a barge—I dance for some sailors—I go to Somerset—The schoolmaster—I am sent to London—The beginning of adventures.

TIDAL BASIN, where I was born, and spent most of the single-figure years of my life, is as everyone knows, one of the poorest and most squalid districts in London. At the time when I can first remember, my father had already left us, convinced, I suppose, that having begotten four children, nothing further could reasonably be expected of a man. And even the law failed to extract from him any contribution towards our support, although I believe he used to be sent to prison at intervals for refusing to pay anything towards his family's upkeep.

We lived in one room, with a scullery attached, containing a round white copper. The only other furniture consisted of a table, one or two very broken-down cane-bottomed chairs, and a carpet chair in which my mother used to rest of an evening, with a folded ironing-blanket for a cushion. We did not possess a bed, and at night used to sleep on bundles of rags in the various corners of the room.

My mother was half French, and at this time still very good-looking. Not more than five feet in height —I am no taller—she had a rich olive complexion and beautiful dark eyes set very wide apart, which I have also inherited. Her nose, however, was better than mine, being a delicate aquiline, whereas mine is, to be honest, rather a snub. Her life must have been a hard one. She had four children to bring up on a total income of ten shillings a week. And to earn this meagre sum she had to work twelve hours a day at a chocolate factory. It would have been excusable if she had neglected us. The amount of work she had to do in the course of the day was simply awful, for I am afraid that as a family we needed a good deal of looking after. I suppose we inherited this from our father. But so long as my mother's strength held out she never surrendered. Although ten shillings a week was not enough to keep us warm and well fed, she at least persevered in keeping us and our home clean. Only the black-beetles escaped all her efforts. I shall never forget the sensation of crushing them under my bare feet. They used to give a sort of scrunch.

Sometimes, but not often, she was able to bring us back some chocolate from the factory. Oh! the delight of that chocolate! It was almost worth being half-starved to enjoy it as we did.

I have only one more recollection of these very early days, and that is of a tall bearded man who visited us one winter evening. Ordinarily we should have retired for the night by the time he arrived, but apparently my mother was expecting him, for she kept the lamp burning. I imagine he was a seaman as he wore small gold rings in his ears. He stayed for a long time, and my mother seemed to enjoy his company. Before he went he took me on his knee and played with me.

From this time onwards he always used to come and see us when his ship was in port, and we got quite used to him. I was always his favourite and he never played with any of the others. His nickname for me was "The little flea," on account, I suppose, of my small size and great quickness of body and mind.

When we were a little older my brother and I used to be sent round to my grandmother's house every Monday morning to fetch the vegetables for our weekly pot of soup. This was rather an event in our lives. Not only was it the most important meal of the week but also one never quite knew what sort of a mood my grandmother might be in. Anything might happen. My grandmother was a remarkable woman, a real coster. Her hair, which she always wore heavily greased and drawn straight back in a tight little knot at the back of her head, was as white as her invariably clean apron. Her face was equally white, making her eyes appear very conspicuous. My brother called her "two holes burnt in a blanket," and infuriated her by calling this after her in the street and running away before she could catch him. She was a really great character and people were very afraid of her.

I often used to walk with her to the market. As soon as we got there we used to go into a pub, where she bought me the same drink as she was having herself—usually either gin or porter. Then came the actual marketing, after which we had another drink and returned home, my grandmother carrying all her purchases folded up in her apron.

It was at my grandmother's house that I first came in contact with death. She lived on the first floor. Below her was a household consisting of a man, his wife, and his sister-in-law. One day my grandmother told me to go down and borrow some milk from them. I knocked at the door. There was no reply. I cautiously opened the door and, looking in, I saw the wife suspended by a stocking from a hook on the door leading into the bedroom. Her face was purple and her eyes bulged like a fish's. It was rather an awful sight, and in spite of things I have seen since then it has always remained firmly fixed in my memory. I can see the body hanging there as if I had only gone into the house and seen it a few days ago. It is extraordinarily vivid to me.

"Can you lend grandma a bottle of milk?" I asked, not knowing how else to attract her attention.

When she made no reply I was rather frightened, and thinking she must be ill, ran upstairs to tell my grandmother. Her reception of the news disappointed me very much. Instead of being treated with the respect due to what I was beginning to think must be important news, I was sent packing, and told not to say anything about what I had seen to anybody. Of course I told everybody I met, but as none of them could give me any satisfactory explanation I decided to ask my mother as soon as she came home. To my intense disappointment she behaved in the same evasive way as my grandmother had done. I was not, however, even at that age, so easily put off, and I soon found out the facts of the story, which were as follows. The wife was expecting a child and had moved into the front room for the period of her confinement. The husband, deprived of her, turned to his sister-in-law, who did not refuse him. By reason of the limited accommodation at their disposal it was not long before the wife's suspicions were aroused, and one day not long before her delivery was expected, hearing what she took to be suspicious sounds in the adjoining room, she arose, investigated, and discovered them. So great, apparently, was the shock of realizing this double infidelity that, unable any longer to endure such a world, she decided to leave it rather than bring another life into it.

Although it did not always end in suicide, this sort of episode was fairly common I discovered as I began to grow up. I think it gives you some sort of idea of the squalor and misery in which I was brought up, and for this reason I look upon it as important.

My grandmother, I have said, was a real coster woman, and the strain of coster blood I inherit from her has had a big effect in moulding my personality. I am a true coster in my flamboyance and my love of colour, in my violence of feeling and its immediate response in speech and action. Even now I am often caught with a sudden longing regret for the streets of Limehouse as I knew them, for the girls with their gaudy shawls and heads of ostrich feathers like clouds in a wind, and the men in their caps, silk neckerchiefs and bright yellow pointed boots in which they took such pride. I adored the swagger and the showiness of it all.

My brother and I used to explore together the remotest parts of Greenwich and Chinatown, often returning very late at night, much to the irritation of my mother, who wanted to rest after her day's work. She often scolded us, but we didn't care, and returned probably even later the following night. There were extraordinary things to be seen in the narrow streets by the river. I suppose it was really a suitable early training for me. It taught me that you could never know what was going to happen next.

I was, I must admit, a good deal frightened of my brother, and my rebellion was partly due to his threats, which he was never afraid to carry out. If ever I showed any sign of refusing to do what he wanted he would pinch me till I gave in, or push me into a canal. On one occasion, however, I had my revenge on him. It was a hot day and we had walked down to one of those Greenwich streets, where there are many little tributaries of the Thames. He was hot and tired, and, thinking it would be pleasant, took off his boots (the only pair in the family) and waded into the water. As soon as he was out of reach I picked up the boots and threw them out into the middle of the stream. They floated a short way and then sank.

My mother was furious when he returned without the boots, and asked him what he had done with them. He naturally told her that I had thrown them into the river. I, however, said that he had thrown them at me standing on the bank and missed. Despite his furious denial of this, she believed me. I was always her favourite. Then she gave him a halfpenny and sent him out to buy a cane. He, knowing the use to which it would be put, spent the halfpenny on sweets and stayed out till after midnight. I had never seen my mother so angry. Our escapades must have been getting on her nerves. As soon as he came in (without the cane) she seized him by the collar and beat him with the rolling-pin till he yelled. It was one of the moments of my life.

But delighted though I was personally with my success, I could not help seeing that the loss of the boots had just tipped the balance so far as my mother was concerned. Her powers of resistance were finished. It was therefore no surprise when one morning a few days later my brother and I were sent to my father with a note explaining that henceforward we should have to live with him.

This was the first sight I had of my father. He was lying on a filthy couch half covered with a rug. As we came in he propped himself surlily on one elbow. He was wearing a collarless grey shirt and leather braces, I remember. His face was almost fleshless, and the working of his loose-lipped mouth had creased the tightly-drawn skin from his temples to his jawbone. His eyes were light blue, rather crazy and dangerous-looking, and very bloodshot. His right eyebrow was almost obliterated by a scar which kept the eye beneath it unnaturally open. He looked absolutely devilish. I was terrified of him and dreaded what our life was going to be like here. I wished

I had behaved a little better to my mother, who then might have kept us with her. I now realized how silly I had been.

At the foot of the couch sat a huge dark Jewess, whose one-time beauty was obvious. She was now enormously fat and shiny, though she was still a fine looking woman. She evidently resented our intrusion, and as soon as she had learnt who we were she advised my father to "send the little bastards to the workhouse."

His retort was to get up from the couch and floor her with a fierce blow in the stomach. Then leaving her to recover, he turned to us and said: "So your mother has sent you to live with me?"

We told him this was so, and it was settled.

The atmosphere of the house was very different from that of our previous home. We were never "allowed" in any other part of the house than the room in which we first saw our father. Day and night we heard people going up and down stairs on some mysterious business which we rightly imagined was being intentionally kept from us. Later I discovered that the place was a brothel run by the Jewess Sarah, on the proceeds of which my father lived and drank in idleness.

The actual conditions of life were much the same here. We had if anything less to eat, and we slept, or tried to sleep, as before on bundles of rags in the corners of the room. In winter my brother and I used to huddle together for warmth. Dreadful was the nipping of hungry bugs, and the cough of an unknown consumptive who always slept in the opposite corner to me. In the summer the stench and stuffiness were such that, although it was strictly forbidden, I used to sneak out and sleep on the stairs, where it was cooler. It was pretty hard sleeping there and you were quite often disturbed by people coming in late and falling over you, but the breath of fresh air which you got there made it worth while facing the discomforts. The first time my father found me there he gave me a long lecture—I honestly believe he felt he was doing something towards redeeming a misspent life by keeping his children from knowledge of evil—and threatened, if he caught me there again, to whip me with an engineer's steel foot-rule that he was carrying. I disregarded his threat, thinking that bully though he was he would not whip me. The next time he caught me, however, he was in a less sentimental stage of drunkenness and carried out his threat.

He was naturally cruel, and when drunk, as he usually was, he became a fiend. One of his favourite amusements was to set our two dogs, Nigger and Rags, to fight one another. Or if he saw a cat in the street he liked to pick it up by its tail and crash out its brains against a wall. The one virtue he both possessed and respected was bravery. He feared no man in Limehouse, and in certain moods he would go out into the street and shout, "Come out, you ——s and fight." Only one man ever answered the challenge, and he had to be taken to the hospital in an ambulance. He trained my brother to be like himself. When only eight years old he was beaten in a fight by a much larger gipsy boy and came home crying to my father, who cursed him for a bloody snivelling little coward, and told him that if he did not go back and fight the gipsy boy till he beat him he would get a far worse hiding at home. My brother went back and thrashed the gipsy boy. When he returned with the news, my father simply shook him by the hand.

By trade my father was a mechanic, but since he had come to live with Sarah he had not found it necessary to do any work. He would just sit about all day drinking and smoking, and if possible picking quarrels with anyone he came across and who was prepared to have a row with him. Previously he had been employed as a fitter in a gas works, and he was so good and quick a workman that he had retained his job in spite of his periodic disappearances. Any kind of regularity, however, he hated. His parents, and my grand-parents therefore, were a cook and a policeman, who had several times tried to put him in the position of making a settled livelihood. Of the fact that his father was a policeman (he became an inspector eventually) I shall tell you more in a moment. It was a most unfortunate thing for my father. Once at his request they had bought him a fried fish business, for which they paid fifty pounds. He ran it for two days, and on the third sold it, stock and all, for a pound. Another time they bought him a fruit barrow for five pounds, and he sold it for half a crown. I am rather like him in money matters.

My removal from Limehouse was very sudden and rather a shock. I was awakened in the middle of the night by the sound of someone banging on the door. It was pitch dark. I huddled into my corner, covered myself with the rags I had been lying on, and kept perfectly still, hoping I should not be noticed. Then I heard a match being struck and a voice inquiring for my father. I was sweating with terror. Deliberate footsteps approached the corner where my brother was sleeping, and the voice said, "Do you know where Father is, sonny?"

"No," came my brother's piping reply. "Maybe he's upstairs."

The footsteps went away and the door was shut. But the lamp was left burning, so I knew that the business, whatever it was, was not finished yet.

"Who was he?" I whispered to my brother.

"A copper," he whispered back.

"What does he want Dad for?"

"I don't know."

We waited for a few minutes. Nothing happened, though we heard the policeman's steps. Then there was a bit of a scuffle and we heard someone swearing at the top of their voice.

The door opened again and the copper re-entered, leading my father, protesting violently, by the arm. My father was wearing handcuffs. It was only then that I saw who the policeman was. It was my grandfather, who was an inspector of police. He had warned my father over and over again that this would happen unless he turned over a new leaf and now it had come to this. He had been sent to arrest him. It was an extraordinary thing to happen.

My grandfather told us to get up and dress, which was unnecessary, as we always slept in our clothes. He was very gentle with us, and said we should be quite all right, but we must come along with him. He then took me by the hand, gripping my father's arm with his other, and led us out into the street. We made a lot of noise going down stairs. Our footsteps sounded very loud. My grandfather's firm and heavy, my father's shuffling and reluctant, though he did not actually try to get away, my brother's quicker, my own tiny ones pattering and timid. They must have sounded very funny.

At last we came to a building with a blue lamp over the door, into which we were told to go. Inside we were separated, and I was taken to a cell with quite a comfortable bed in it, and locked up for the night. I soon went to sleep.

Next morning they brought me a cup of tea and some bread and margarine—the nicest food I had ever tasted. At ten o'clock we were brought before the magistrate. I did not understand what the discussion was about, but one of the incidents of the trial was that my grandmother, who was the only person my father was at all afraid of, was so angry with him for bringing public disgrace on the family that she rushed up to him and hit him hard over the head with the thick rolled umbrella she always carried. There was a frightful scene I remember. I heard the magistrate say, "And the little girl can go to her grandmother's."

This was my other grandmother—my father's mother. I was handed over to her as soon as the case ended. But instead of keeping me she sent me to an aunt and her husband, with whom I lived on a barge for the next few years.

My father, I heard later, was sentenced to two years' imprisonment, after which he and his twin brother went out to Canada, and joined the mounted police, where they gained credit for their bravery. When the war broke out my father joined the first Canadian contingent that came over here. He never got to the front, however, where he would probably have done well, but catching a chill while in training on Salisbury Plain he died of double pneumonia.

My life now changed completely. It became much duller for a bit, but it was also a good deal more comfortable. I was properly fed and looked after. However, I am not sure that I was really grateful for the change.

All day long my uncle used to sit grasping the tiller in one hand and the bowl of his short-stemmed clay pipe in the other, with his eyes fixed in a very firm stare on some point a few feet above the beautifully carved green and yellow figurehead, as if he were slowly considering whether it was worth while recollecting all his adventures—though his meditations were more probably concerned with the question of dinner. The stream brushed the sides of the boat as slowly as can be imagined, and the landscape always seemed to be the same. Sometimes I wondered whether I should ever get away from these rivers and canals and see the life that must be going on in the world on shore.

I was a little brown-faced marmoset, dressed in a starched white frock, and the only quick thing in this very slow world. I skipped about, getting in my aunt's way in the tiny kitchen, or else dirtied my clothes and myself by playing among the cargo, and generally I was getting into trouble in some way or another.

My aunt and uncle were, I suppose, very kind to me. They washed me a good deal, forbade me to use certain words, brushed my hair far longer than I thought necessary, insisted on me cleaning my teeth twice a day, and taught me the Lord's Prayer.

"The poor child," I once heard my aunt say, "has had no proper unbringing. She's a regular little savage." My nature, however, was then as now not very tractable to "improvement." I have never wanted to be different from what I am, and have jealously repelled or fled from any influence that seemed likely to alter my personality. I chafed under the restraints and monotony of life on the barge, and was for a time sulky and miserable. My aunt and uncle took no notice of me.

This feeling of neglect reached a climax one evening when we had moored for the night after unloading our cargo at a wharf near Chelsea. I had been ashore—a rare pleasure—and had spent the few pence I possessed on a scarlet handkerchief, which I tied round my head, and which I felt sure looked very becoming. On returning to the barge I ran up to my aunt to show it to her, saying, "Don't you think it's pretty?" She looked up from her work crossly and replied, "What? That thing on your head? Don't be so silly." I stamped out of the cabin in tears. Nobody cared a bit about me. I didn't matter. I would run away and find some people who did, which would be easy. Of that I had no doubt. I knew I was not destined to live and die unnoticed. I knew even then that my life was not to be an ordinary one.

And so I went to sleep, bitter and miserable. However, as it happened, I was on the point of discovering that everybody did not think like my aunt and uncle. I was going for the first time to take a real line of my own.

The next morning I was surprised, on looking out of the minute window, to see that a big ship had drawn up alongside us during the night. I dressed, put on my despised headdress, and went out to look at it. As soon as I emerged a bunch of sailors on the deck called down to me, "Hullo, kid." Then some impulse or other urged me to dance for them. I had never danced before, but it came quite easily to me. They were delighted, and threw me pennies. I danced more and more, and even sang, and they threw down more pennies, and at last a sixpence or two. They were enthusiastic about my performance. I was delighted. At last someone seemed to understand and appreciate me. Perhaps life was not going to be so bad after all.

After this I would always dance whenever we were near a ship, which happened quite fairly often, and, as all sailors seemed to like watching me dance, soon I became quite well known up and down the river.

Some time after this—I really cannot remember exactly how old I was when various things happened—it was decided that a start ought to be made with my education. I was sent to another aunt, who had a farm in Somerset, and for the next few years I attended the village school.

I do not think I managed to learn very much there. In fact lessons rather bored me, but even here I got to know more about life, and it was from here that I was to start off on my real career.

This country existence was as strange to me as I myself no doubt was to the people I found myself among. For a week or so I found it lovely. To be awakened by the crowing of cocks, to open my eyes upon fruit trees gently swaying against a blue sky, to dress, eat a large breakfast (bits of straw still sticking to the egg shells) and then proceed down the path which divided the oats from the barley, and across the wide village green where the ducks quacked round my ankles, to the village school standing next to the church. I entered joyously into the reality of what I now know was a childish dream. I played my part as happily, as wholly, as singly and as passionately as only those can who half know they are playing a part. I dangled my sun-bonnet by its strings. I stuck poppies and daisies in my hair. I was plump and brown and healthy. Two boys from the grammar-school fell in love with me.

I always went about attended by a contingent of grammar-school boys. They were for the most part older than I, but they had not had my experience. I was the acknowledged leader. What games we had! What scrapes I led them into!—always escaping the blame myself on the ground of being only a little girl. I taught them to get drunk on cider, and when they became accustomed to that I stole my aunt's burgundy and filled the bottle up with water. These things may sound rather silly, but I think they show the direction which I was going to take, and for this reason they rather amuse me to remember and to tell you about.

One of our most amusing exploits was my revenge on a priggish little girl called Edith, the chemist's daughter, who told tales about me to the schoolmistress. Her parents were very proud of her, and every Sunday used to dress her up in the most elaborate frocks, with huge sashes and hair ribbons to match. I thought of something. I went out and bought a packet of drummer dyes which I dissolved in a large rainwater butt. Then I detailed some of my cavaliers to isolate and capture the little beribboned horror, whom we immersed, finery and all, in the mixture I had prepared. We left her screaming and clinging to the edge of the butt, and withdrew to enjoy her struggles. At length she had to give up calling for help that showed no signs of being forthcoming, and to climb out by her own efforts, derisively encouraged by her tormentors. Her appearance when she did eventually emerge, an awful, bedraggled mess, weeping indigo tears, and spluttering threats of the penalties she would see were inflicted on us, was a sight on which any inhabitant of this sad world could close his eyes with a contented sigh.

The years passed in this way, and without knowing it I began to grow up. I suppose in a way this time in the country was a happy one. Nothing much happened, but then I did not expect anything much to happen. It was a sort of rest to prepare me for the sort of thing that was to come. One of the masters of the grammar-school had meanwhile been taking an interest in me. We met for the first time outside the school gate, where I was waiting for my friends to come out. He was a youngish man with a clean-shaven florid face and a large letter-box of a mouth, through which he uttered slightly facetious remarks in a clipped and, to me, unfamiliar accent. He always wore grey flannel trousers, a tight-fitting cloth cap, and a sports coat with sleeves that looked about an inch and a half too short. But although his manner was outwardly rather domineering and patronizing, I felt that he was sad. He might have been ambitious in his boyhood, or perhaps he might have been in love, though this seemed impossible to me. But whatever he may have longed for, I felt sorry for him. With me he seemed to be able to recover for the moment some of his lost dreams.

For my part I learned a great deal from him. He was one of the first cultured men I had ever met, and I naturally love culture. He used to take me for long walks on Sundays, during which with infinite patience he would try to reveal to me spiritual pleasures of which I had never before had an inkling. For this odd man had an enthusiasm for Keats, and knew nearly all his poems by heart. It must have been pleasant for him to find a sympathetic, if not well-read, listener.

For a long time we used to go about together. The understanding between us grew more and more strong. I can hardly say, in the light of what I have learnt since, that we were in love. At least perhaps he was. Certainly I was fond of him. And thus things went on until we were more intimate than my aunt and the rest of the village gossips thought proper. I see now looking back on it that

[Basil.

BETTY MAY

it was a relationship that could not last. I do not think either of us was altogether to blame. After all, he was lonely. There was no one in the neighbourhood he could meet on equal terms or whom he could talk to about the things he loved. I myself at this time had not been very happy with the people I knew. I longed for a bigger life, and I felt that such a life did really exist somewhere if only I could get to it. By his conversation this man had shown me something of a world I had hardly dreamed of. But none of this was considered to be of any account by everyone else. There was a great deal of fuss, and it was made clear to me that unless the friendship came to an end it would be the schoolmaster who would be made to suffer. I did not take all this lying down, but I could not do anything to prevent it. The result was that after a rather tearful scene with my aunt I was packed off with a few pounds to make a start in life somewhere else. And so in sorrow and not a little fear I found myself one day in the train bound once more for London.

What did I think of on that journey? Did I reflect—after I had produced my ticket—that the departing landscape (I forget whether it was summer or winter, or harvest or seed-time) was perhaps symbolic of lost innocence? Did I realize that I had finally cast off the comfortable shackles of childhood, and was being whirled, as the novelists say, at the rate of sixty miles an hour—why always sixty miles an hour?—towards London, into whose midst I should so soon be helplessly sucked? I wish I could remember the answers to these questions, but I have really forgotten, and so if I want my readers to believe in the truth of these memoirs I will not try to imagine these things but will just admit this fact to them. Certainly I suppose I ought to have been thinking on these lines, and those who happen to read this book may take it that I actually did so—which is, after all, as likely as not. If they so desire, let them be assured, too, that the ticket collector was a fat man with a squint, who had a wife and three children at home, and advised me where to go when I arrived in London.

He may indeed have done so for all I can remember, since it is certain that I should not have taken his advice. In a way I was rather excited to be on my own at last. I now knew that I was in for some adventure. I did not know where I should find it, but I felt pretty sure that it would appear soon. I went, as it happens, straight to the Commercial Road, a district I had been familiar with before I went to the country, where I immediately bought myself some "grown up" clothes, a skirt that would have touched the ankles of the person it was designed for—worn by me it not only threatened to trip me up at every step, but was in serious danger of slipping off altogether—and a monstrous hat, trimmed rather like an old-fashioned ship under full sail, which the secondhand dealer assured me was exactly how hats were being worn at Ascot and Goodwood that year.

Thus arrayed, I stumbled out into the street, clutching anxiously at the folds of my absurd skirt with one hand, and with the other continually feeling for the small sum of money with which I had to make my start in life without further help from others, to assure myself that it was still there—a comical sight. For a long time I wandered about, not knowing what to do or how to get a room, until I encountered a young Jew, who took me into a pub and gave me a gin, the first I had had since going to the market with my grandmother, many years before. In the pub a kindly woman asked me how old I was, and offered to take me home with her to sleep. I gladly availed myself of her compassion, but could not bring myself to tell even her the reason why I had come to London.

This was a real bit of luck, of course. Goodness knows what would have happened to me if this woman had not looked after me at that moment. As it was, although I was not with her for long, I got used to being in London and became more full of confidence.

A short time later my protectress was compelled for business reasons to leave me in a public house with some friends, who promised to see me home. A well-dressed man, however, came in shortly after she had left, who showed a good deal of interest in me and offered to take me to the West End. I am never able to resist adventure, and against the advice of my friends I consented to go with him.

Their advice was justified by his conduct as soon as he got me alone in a taxi. I was terrified. I resisted him in all the ways I could think of. I fought and scratched, and I did not scruple to bite. Failing in the direct physical attack, he fell back upon persuasion—a stage in the winning of a woman which I gather he had in his previous experience found it possible to do without. He pointed out all the advantages, the clothes, the dinners, the good times, I should gain from an association with himself. But I was not moved. He sketched the squalor and poverty in which he had found me, and from which he intended to remove me, but I was not grateful. He then abused me for a lousy little slut, who ought to be left to wallow in my own filth. I replied by asking him why he would not permit me to return to it. This infuriated him. He stormed and threatened, and lastly, as a climax, declared that he loved me.

As I have indicated, and as the reader will easily believe, I was not at this time in a mood to enjoy love-making. Fear can turn every prospect and glamour of romance to mud, and I was frightened. Consequently his abasement won no more from me than his assaults or his bribes or his abuse or his threats had done. I hated the sight of him and told him so. I wondered why men would not leave one alone. They were all right at first when they offered to show one life, and then at once they became a nuisance.

This, or something like it, must, I think, have been the reasoning that led him to the course of action I am about to describe. I suppose he thought that whatever he was going to get out of me would only be got after a great deal of trouble, and quite likely not at all. He probably did not like people like that, and so that was why he acted as he did.

The taxi stopped in what I found out later to be Leicester Square. My companion assisted me to get out and led me by the arm to the door of a club—now extinct—situated close to where the Café Anglais now stands, on the east side of the Square.

"Are you sure you wouldn't like to come in?" he asked, while we waited for the attendant to appear in answer to our summons.

"I suppose I'll have to," I said more sulkily than ever.

"Are you sure you couldn't love me?"

Before I could answer, the fanlight was illuminated and the door opened, revealing a flight of uncarpeted stairs, up which floated sounds of music, dancing, chatter, and the chinking of glasses. I describe the scene in detail, because the next moment, without any warning, he pushed me down the stairs and went away, banging the door behind him.

CHAPTER II

THE CAFÉ ROYAL

My first night club—Rosie's wig—A Cambridge undergraduate—
The Endell Street Club—I am taken to the Café
Royal—Epstein—Augustus John—Horace Cole—Epstein
speaks to me—The Cave of the Golden Calf—Madame
Strindberg—"The Cherub"—"Pretty Pet"—I go to Bordeaux.

THE episode I have just related, or to be more accurate
am in the middle of relating, is a good starting-point for
the next phase of my story. The door through which I had
been thrown so violently, shut with a loud bang before
I came to rest at the bottom of the stairs, and you can
imagine my consternation when I looked upwards to find
my pursuer had disappeared.

Awakened by that bang to my senses I looked up
and around and surveyed a new world containing no
familiar figure—not even his who had been responsible
for flinging me there. Next I proceeded to investigate in
greater detail the people and the surroundings among
which I had been marooned.

This was my first sight of a life that I was afterwards
to know so well. In the corner a band was playing, and on
a shiny floor couples were dancing. The place was simply
packed with people, and the atmosphere was very thick
with smoke. Everybody seemed to be talking at once. I

37

felt quite dazed and rather frightened, and did not in the least know what to do with myself. I was of course in a night club, but I had hardly heard of such a thing in those days and I certainly never expected to find myself in one. Anyway I had not thought beforehand that I should suddenly be literally thrown head-first into one.

Entering the room at the end of a dance I saw only one vacant chair, on which, after politely obtaining the permission of the man at whose table it was placed, I sat down. My intrusion, or more probably the interest the man showed in me, aroused the resentment of his female companion. She began by taking advantage of my ignorance to try to make me appear ridiculous, but I was not even then to be made fun of so easily. My wits were far sharper than hers, and I soon discomforted her. Irritated by her failure, she became insulting. My nostrils dilated, as they do when I am angry, but still she dared to jeer at me. This went on for some time. The man was quite nice and talked to me kindly, but she kept on interrupting and being as rude to me as she could. I tried to make up my mind what to do. At length she got up and danced with the man, who would no doubt have preferred to remain at the table, and as they passed by where I was sitting she looked backwards at me over her shoulder. " She's a pretty little thing, but it's a pity she has false teeth! "

She said that I—I—had false teeth! This was more than I could endure. I jumped up and slapped her as hard as I could on the face. Shocked waiters immediately bundled us upstairs into the street, fighting all the time. I meant to make her pay dearly for that insult. False teeth indeed! I would strangle her for it. No, on second thoughts I would catch her by the hair and smash her face so that she would never attract another man—that would be a better revenge I decided, and I had begun to put this plan into execution. I plunged my fingers into her hair and pulled hard, but the result was not what I expected. I found myself lying in the gutter, and clutched in my right hand—I could hardly believe my eyes—was a chestnut wig.

All my anger against her died down on the instant as I saw her standing there, hairless as a worm. Seldom have I seen a funnier sight, and never a woman so thoroughly humiliated. I must say that after this happened she behaved very well. Instead of being angry, she asked for her wig back and crammed it on to her head, telling me to say nothing about it and asking me to go back to the club with her. After this she was very kind.

When I had done laughing, I returned her the wig, and Rosie and I, for that was her name, went back to the club quite good friends. Soon after this incident she married a young man and went out with him to New Zealand, where they bought a farm out of her savings, and are, I believe, living happily to this day. But I often wonder if he has yet discovered that she wears a wig.

This was really my introduction to the world that I was going to live in for the future, and in many ways I suppose it showed me the sort of thing I was in for. Anyway it turned out that the incident I have just told you about was all for the best.

From this time on I began to find my feet. Rosie

helped me to find a room, and I found that after paying
for it I could still afford to buy myself some clothes. In
the choice of these I was able to show for the first time the
flamboyant taste in colour that I inherit from my coster
ancestry. I could only afford one outfit, but every item of
it was of a different colour. Neither red nor green nor blue
nor yellow nor purple was forgotten, for I loved them
all equally, and if I was not rich enough to wear them
separately, rather than be parted from any one of them,
I would wear them, like Joseph in the Bible, all at once!
Colours to me are like children to a loving mother. Each
is my favourite, yet I can never bring myself to deny the
others by preferring one.

It is very irritating to me that I who always know
my own mind should be to this day unable to come to a
decision upon this matter. It is too bad. But I always feel
that I have got my own back when I wear all colours at
once. Few people, you will find, if you read this book to
the end, can boast of having come off best in competition
with Betty May!

Dressed then in the brilliant colours that are my right
and heritage, my personality burst suddenly forth in its
full peculiarity. From this moment I felt I was grown up
and after the experiences I had had I could now start
life. As I looked at myself in the mirror after my latest
purchases, in my new finery I felt I was now ready to
descend upon the expectant world.

The person, however, who was really responsible for
discovering me and taking me to the scenes of my future
life was a nice-looking boy from Cambridge, whom I

shall refer to as Gerald. I was standing one night outside the Holborn Empire watching the people and feeling very lonely when he came up and spoke to me.

"Would you like to go in?" he asked.

"Yes," I said, "I'd love to."

So he took me in to see the show and afterwards we made great friends. As I found him kind and well off, we saw a lot of each other and often went out together. He was charming, and I used to amuse him a great deal by both my knowledge and ignorance of the world which always seemed to him such an extraordinary mixture. I began to get the fever of night life in my blood. And wherever we went people wondered who was the girl with long plaits who dressed so oddly.

Among other places, we frequented the Endell Street Club, a favourite resort of journalists before the war. It was here that I met Jack C——, an American over here on a visit, who was to take me for the first time to the Café Royal. He was greatly intrigued with me at first sight, and I liked his appearance. It turned out that he was a great help to me. I was, I remember, very depressed after seeing Gerald off on the way back to Cambridge, and could not endure the prospect of going back to the place where he had arranged for me to be looked after while he was away. He had made me promise not to go out to night clubs alone, but I didn't care. I dislike solitude, and if he had understood me he would not have exacted such a promise.

Reasoning thus, I went straight from the terminus to the Endell Street Club. Jack was there and asked me to meet him at the Café Royal the following night.

THE OLD CAFÉ ROYAL. BY ADRIAN ALLINSON

I remember there was a very lovely German woman who used to be at the Endell Street Club a great deal. She was always beautifully dressed and covered with sparkling jewels. She always used to make me, with my two long plaits, feel very young and unimportant. (By the way, I used to put these plaits up under my hat before going into the Club, but they usually came down in the course of the evening.) One evening I was standing beside this beautiful German, and I asked her straight out how she came by all her fine clothes.

"Would you like some?" she said.

She then explained to me that she earned her living by blackmail. She gave me a complete description of how she worked. She suggested that I should join her, saying that my appearance and childlike looks would be very useful in her profession. I was terribly shocked and upset by all this. In spite of what I had seen in the way of vice and crime this seemed different somehow. Anyhow, I was very rude to her and we never spoke again.

The old Café Royal was a very different sort of place from the new one. It was, to begin with, a real café. There was sawdust all over the floor and none except marble-topped tables. The gilded decorations were as gaudy and as bright as possible. The drinks were quite cheap. I cannot describe them more accurately than that, and must rely on the memories of those of my readers who, like me, knew and loved the Café as it then was. I find now that I am always meeting people who never knew the Café as it was in the old days. They always talk of it and think of it as the rather grand place it is to-day.

I had never seen anything like it. The lights, the mirrors, the red plush seats, the eccentrically dressed people, the coffee served in glasses, the pale cloudy absinthe. I was ravished by all these and felt as if I had strayed by accident into some miraculous Arabian palace.

Though Jack, who knew the Café well, could not understand my enthusiasm, he agreed readily to take me there again, and partly out of gratitude and partly to make sure that he kept his promise, I always went about with him while Gerald was at Cambridge.

No duck ever took to water, no man to drink, as I to the Café Royal. The colour and the glare, the gaiety and the chatter appealed to something fundamental in my nature. I took to going there nearly every day, even if Jack could not come with me. I used to sit at a table by myself, with a cheap drink, coffee or lager, in front of me to justify my presence, my head resting in both my hands, watching the parties of artists and models at the top end of the room. I knew only a few of their names, although I soon got to know them all by sight. They were objects of positive sanctity to me. I never imagined for a moment that anyone noticed me at all. However, it turned out later that they did, and no one was more surprised than I was to find this out. I used to invent stories for myself about their careless, wild, generous way of life. I tried to imagine what it must be like to be made love to by one of those great men, and I envied the models who were privileged to sit with them and listen to their conversation (whose probable brilliance soared above all the efforts of my fancy), and, of course, to be their lovers. How I longed to be allowed even a sip from those fountains of wisdom!

I arranged these marvellous beings in my imagination into a sort of order, of which Epstein, with his massive benignity and his mild eyes, was the topmost point. They became part of my life, and although I did not actually pray to them, they were as important to me as the gods of any religion could be. Augustus John particularly intrigued me. In those days of course he was not the famous man he is now, though even then he was obviously a great man. He always wore a black hat, cloak, neckerchief, etc., and would usually sit without speaking except to give a periodic gruff order for another whisky and soda. Allinson was another who had no fear of the picturesque and dressed invariably in a velvet coat and a large stock. He used to play the piano marvellously with his long, sensitive fingers, and he had a wonderful white horse on which he would sometimes ride back to his house in the early hours of the morning. He was also said to possess a wonderful Chinese bed of incredible value. And Roger Fry, the art critic, Nina Hamnett, whose drawings are now becoming famous—a very good one of me by her is reproduced in this book—Bomberg, with his great head of red hair, his red beard, and big blue eyes, Ian Strang, J. D. Innes, Rowley Smart (later an old friend of mine), Odell, to name only a few, helped to complete the picture. All the medical students in those days used to wear side-whiskers and big, black, floppy bow ties. One of the most amusing of them was Barry Hyde. Afterwards he became quite a celebrated doctor, but he is now dead.

The handsomest of the models was, in my opinion, Lilian Shelley. And above all there was Horace Cole, the great hoaxer. His practical jokes have now become so famous that he is almost a legendary figure, but he does really exist and is still to be seen. Most of his hoaxes are world-famous, but you will remember how he was received by the officers and men of a famous battleship with full naval honours under the impression, created of course by himself, that he was an Eastern potentate. On another occasion he and some friends arrived in Piccadilly dressed as workmen, and proceeded to pick the road up, in which condition it remained for some time. Another time he had a certain very famous person arrested for stealing his watch, to that famous person's great surprise. In fact, there is no end to the stories about him.

Now I have told you of my distant, day-dreaming adoration of these Bohemian divinities you will find it easy to feel the rapture, the ecstasy of joy and fear that I felt when invited to go over and join them at their table. I was sitting, as I have described, with my chin cupped in my hands and my remarkable face framed in my black hair, alone, an intriguing object I suppose, in a way, when to my amazement and consternation I saw Epstein look at me, get up from his place, and walk towards me. At first I thought he must be going to speak to a friend at some table behind mine, but no, he held undeterred on his course. He was really coming to Me. I was too frightened to smile or to say anything polite. I could only stare at him. But as soon as he spoke my fear departed.

"You're very young to be here, little girl, aren't you?" he said, and I smiled trustfully back.

Then he asked me to come and sit at his table. You can imagine how delighted and excited I was. Of course after that I met everybody of any importance at all who came to the Café, as Epstein knew absolutely everybody there was to know. And this was the manner of my introduction to the Bohemian fraternity.

For about a year I played the part of the baby and mascot of the Café Royal set. I sat for several artists, but not for Epstein, who thought I was not yet developed enough to be interesting as material for his particular style of modelling. And I did some of my songs and dances at the Cabaret Club, or as it was called later "the Cave of the Golden Calf," our usual resort after the Café Royal, the proprietress of which, Madame Strindberg, was one of the most remarkable characters of those times.

It was here that I met a charming man whom I will tell you about. Some people will remember him, as he was quite a character I afterwards discovered and was to be seen everywhere.

I had just finished a song there one night and was resuming my seat amidst applause when I found myself being spoken to by an old gentleman whose clothes and appearance seemed very unsuitable for the Cabaret Club. The dress of St. James's Street looked very odd in front of Epstein's very funny frescoes on the walls of the club. But he gave no sign of embarrassment, and drank beer out of a china mug as easily as if it had been vintage port or Napoleon brandy. His assurance won my admiration. He had followed me, it appeared, from the Café Royal out of wonder at my extreme youth. I was delighted with him, and gave him a not entirely untrue account of my life, remaining none the less very strictly on my guard. I christened him "the Cherub."

After this he became very persistent in his attentions, but our relationship was that of father and daughter, with which he appeared quite satisfied, and gave me, I must say, first class entertainment. We used to dine together nearly every night, and he took great pains to educate my taste in food and drink, of which he was a great connoisseur. I was told that the sauce we were having to-night showed up the deficiencies of the one we had had the night before, or that the soufflé nowhere approached the one of ten days ago. And quite as subtle were the distinctions I was urged to appreciate between the various wines. Like a pupil in music, I strained my intelligence to remember all these things, and at times almost persuaded myself that my taste was as refined as that of my host, which was of course impossible, as my palate was untrained, and from inexperience I had no standards of excellence to refer to for comparisons.

I now see that he thoroughly enjoyed all this pretence and probably exaggerated tremendously to see how far I would really go in pretending to agree with him and air my own knowledge. But for the mere matter of pleasure I am convinced that I enjoyed what I ate quite as keenly as he did, though for less good reasons. Or rather I should have done so had I not feared that, being ignorant of what food ought to taste like, an admission of pleasure might be a confession of vulgarity. It was unlike me to admit any rules other than my own preferences, and I soon defied one of my tutor's most sacred beliefs. In England, as you know, good champagne is dry champagne, and the sweeter varieties are considered fit only for women and Frenchmen. I happen to prefer it sweet. I know it is bad taste, but I cannot help that. I still prefer it sweet just as much as I did in those days. So one night in the Café Royal when we were drinking champagne of especial dryness in honour of some occasion or other, after taking a preliminary sip I commanded the astonished waiter to bring me some sugar! He protested, but I was firm, and beneath the outraged eyes of the Cherub I deliberately dropped first one lump, and then, having tested the effect, another, into the holy fluid. The monocle clattered against the shirt front at each successive blasphemy.

My time was not, however, entirely taken up with the Cherub. I had made another more exciting acquaintance at the Endell Street Club. He was pale, dissolute and smartly dressed, and usually wore several rings on the fingers of his unexpectedly large and powerful, but at the same time white and well-shaped hands. I was attracted to him by his skilful dancing, his garish accounts of life in foreign cities, his lithe brutality and the fear he inspired in everybody, not excluding myself. He was known in England and on the Continent as "Pretty Pet." I knew he had a very bad reputation, but no one seemed to know anything definite about him. It was not known how much money he had or where he got it from, but he always seemed to spend a good deal. He was a mysterious figure.

I used to dance with him at the Endell Street Club nearly every night, shamelessly cutting my engagements with the Cherub. I was fascinated. And when he asked me to go to Bordeaux with him I agreed without a moment's hesitation. He told me he could get me a job as a dancer. Now, I thought, I am going to see life.

We embarked at London Bridge in a tramp steamer, and arrived at Bordeaux three days later, having been delayed by fog.

CHAPTER III

FRANCE

Bordeaux—I dance at a café chantant—I fight with Pretty Pet
and leave him—I am taken on as a professional dancer—
The Apache—I go to Paris—The Apache gang—I fight with
Hortense—"Tiger-Woman"—I fight with The Strangler—
The methods of the gang—The branding—The gang is
dispersed—I return to England.

I REMEMBER that snow was falling hard when we landed
at Bordeaux harbour at 8 a.m. I had eaten practically
nothing while we were at sea, and was almost fainting
with cold and weakness. My unsuitable and very
insufficient clothing was wet through and clung tightly to
my wincing flesh. Added to this, the captain of the tramp
steamer had told me that Pretty Pet was a bad hat. I had
no money to get home with, and I was still a mere child.

We went to the Hôtel Montre, where Pretty Pet
engaged two adjacent rooms with a door between. I had
a hot bath and some food and rested while my clothes
were being dried. By evening I was feeling much happier
and went out with Pretty Pet to a restaurant for dinner
and afterwards to a café chantant. Here we sat for a
time drinking absinthe and grenadine and watching the
performers on a small stage at the far end of the café.
This I enjoyed. I have always loved watching anything

like a cabaret. And then it suddenly occurred to me that I should like to take part in it. I thought about it for some time, feeling rather shy of suggesting it. At length I asked if I might do a dance. Permission was granted and I went up to the stage and danced as I used to dance for the sailors on the Thames. And as I used to at the Cabaret Club. I still had had no lessons, but no one seemed to mind that. Everybody enjoyed watching me dance. I was a great success. I was recalled time and again and given a great many drinks. After I had finished we returned to the hotel and I went to bed feeling very tired.

I had, however, only just switched off the light when the partition door opened and Pretty Pet walked in. Inflamed with drink and leering with befuddled lust, his unattractive countenance (which had, by the way, earned him the title of Pretty Pet) looked unutterably repulsive. I think I took the situation in pretty well. I at once switched on the light and made for the dressing-table, where I had left my nail scissors—a flimsy enough weapon in all conscience for defence against a desperate White Slaver—for this I had discovered was my cavalier's profession—but it was the best available and proved in my hands sufficient for the purpose. Pretty Pet was too drunk to see me pick up the scissors, which I grasped firmly in my right hand, the points protruding between my first and second fingers, and the handles pressed firmly against the ball of my thumb—and came at me with careless eagerness, not knowing that I had a weapon. I easily eluded his first clumsy attempt to get me in his arms, and ducking, struck upwards and buried the scissors an inch deep in his wrist. Sobered and riled by the pain, he attacked me in real earnest. He clasped me round the waist, pinning both my arms to my sides, and pushed me towards the bed. I struggled with all the strength that fear and hate could give me. He was, of course, much stronger than I was, but I am so small and wiry that he found it difficult to get a proper grip of me and I kept on wriggling out of his clutches. No one in history can have fought more desperately than I did to escape the Pretty Pet. With a supreme effort, just as I felt the edge of the bed against me, I succeeded in half freeing my right arm so that I was enabled to dig my scissors into the fleshy part of his neck. The pain made him relax his hold for a moment, and seizing the opportunity I hit him as hard as I could on the point of the jaw. He fell, and I dashed over to the fireplace (which I had not been able to get at at first because he was between me and it), and fetched a pair of tongs, with which I hit him about the head once or twice to keep him quiet. I then told him that if he moved or spoke I would smash him properly. The threat took effect, for although I made myself comfortable on the bed he did not stir all night from where he lay.

The next morning I ordered him to get back to his own room, and when I had dressed and packed the few things belonging to me I left the hotel and went out into the streets of Bordeaux, speaking practically no French and possessing no money at all. That was the last I saw of "Pretty Pet," but I believe he is dead now. He seems to have died just as much a mystery as he lived, no one knowing who he was or where he came from.

But what a fool I had been! I was so pleased by my victory that I had entirely forgotten to get any money, and now it was too late. As the day wore on my remorse, added to by hunger, became increasingly strong.

Turning the situation over in my mind, I decided that I must immediately set about finding some exployment and a lodging. The first likely plan that came into my head was to apply at the café chantant where I had been such a success the night before. An excellent plan, but alas! I had entirely forgotten the location of the café and was doubtful whether I should be able to recognize it even if by good luck I should happen upon it by chance.

My hunger, however, had to be satisfied, and I went into the first café I saw and boldly ordered coffee and rolls. When the time came for me to pay I told the proprietor that I had no money but offered to work for my meal, and asked him if he would take me on permanently. I will not tell you exactly what he said, but he did not leave me in any doubt as to what he meant. He got an answer he did not expect. I was so angry that I marched indignantly out of the café.

I had walked half the length of the street feeling pleased with my retort before I remembered that my recent way of getting food could not be repeated indefinitely, and that I had as yet found no place wherein to spend the night. I racked my brains to recall something of the appearance of the café I was looking for, and of the features of the street in which it was situated, but without success. I had relied too much on Pretty Pet's guidance. In this repentant frame of mind I stopped and got a clear picture in my mind of the street I was in, with the intention of using it as a starting-point for my further explorations of Bordeaux, which I set out upon at once, reflecting that, lacking as I did money and friends, I had the greater need of such knowledge as I could get hold of. I particularly noted, in addition to the main streets of the town, the bypaths and alley ways, that might prove valuable for throwing off the pursuit of either apaches or gendarmes, or even my late admirer.

I continued my searching until I was too tired to walk further, and then returned into the first cafe that met my eyes. I wondered what on earth I could do. There seemed absolutely no hope of finding anywhere where I could so much as lay my head for the night. Much less get a job. I could not of course pay for a drink, but I could at least sit down until I was turned out, and besides—in spite of my previous experience—I had hopes that I might meet with some kindness.

All cafés, to be sure, bear a family resemblance to each other, but I felt somehow as if I had been in this one before. . . . It wasn't? . . . Could it be? . . . There was the stage—the proprietor. . . . It was! All my troubles were at an end. I rushed up to the proprietor, a kind-looking old man, and said,

"I'm the little girl who danced here last night."

He looked at me, puzzled, and remarked, "Comment?"

"Qui avait dansé," I replied, and gave a brief demonstration.

"Ah, oui!" he exclaimed and clapped his hands.

He was overjoyed to see me again, and gladly agreed

to my proposals, made in awful French, helped by much gesture and illustration, that he should take me on permanently as a dancer and general help.

I was given a meal and allotted a bed in the same room as his little daughter. This was, of course, an amazing stroke of luck. It is this sort of thing that makes me believe in Fate, and from what followed you will see that I have good reason to.

That night my dancing met with even more success than it had the night before, and my delighted employer very kindly gave me a glass of wine to refresh me before I should be called upon again. I drank only half of it before responding to the clamour of the audience, who insisted on an encore. This time I sang to them—in English, for I knew no French songs then—song after song, "The raggle-taggle gipsies," "The Bonny Earl o' Murray," "There lived a girl in Amsterdam," which I had learned at the Cabaret Club just before I left England, "There was an old woman who lived by herself—all in that lonely wood," a nursery rhyme that I had known all my life, and as a final encore, "I know who I love, but the De'il knows who I'll marry," a song which I have always felt a great affection for.

It was at this point that a thing happened which was to alter the whole of my life. It was entirely unexpected and it took such a short time to happen, and events followed in such quick succession, that before I knew where I was my whole life had once more altered completely.

Returning to my table I was surprised to find seated there a man whom I must pause to describe in some

detail, as it was through him that the course of my life
for the next year was to be diverted in a most astonishing
direction. The first and only thing that comes into my
head to compare him with is a sewer rat. He had the
same appearance, and gave the same impression of
narrow-headed meanness and viciousness. What the
comparison does not convey is his air of vanity and
bravado. He wore a seedy black coat, cut in the usual
high-waisted French style, with the collar turned up,
dark blue trousers, pointed brown patent-leather boots,
a scarlet neckerchief, and a light grey cap with a large
peak. He was short and slim—I should put his height at
about five feet seven. His eyes were black and beady, like
those of a rat, and his yellow skin was stretched tightly
over the bones of his face.

"A stage apache," you will say.

"A real apache," I reply, "and therefore an actor."

I was to get to know this in the future. Men who looked
as if they were merely dressed up to look like dangerous
characters *were* actually dangerous characters and used
their appearance to terrify those whom they thought
would be useful to them or whom they blackmailed.

I smiled at him before sitting down, but his features
gave no evidence that he had perceived either me or my
smile. I took up my glass and was about to drink with no
further thought of this surly youth when, before I could
convey it to my lips, he dashed it from my hand.

I slapped his face. There was dead silence, then an
uproar. His expression was the embodiment of every
sneaking, spiteful, cruel, vicious, revengeful passion.

I withdrew under cover of the commotion to a remoter table. But I felt his wicked little eyes follow me through the press. I felt them sticking into my shoulder-blades like red hot pins. Turning my head, I saw he was still intently eyeing me, and looked away with a shudder. The red hot pins again lodged in my shoulder-blades. Which was worse—to look upon him, or to feel him behind me like a fiend about to jump on my back? I could not decide.

For an hour I sat looking at him and away and at him again, and all the time his eyes neither blinked nor diverted their gaze from me for a second so far as I could observe. It was a nerve-fretting experience. At length, like the heroine of a novel, I felt that if I were subjected to this strain a moment longer I should scream. So I walked out of the café, keeping my eyes from him with an effort, and turning either to the right or the left (I forget which), I hurried away as fast as I was able. But in a few yards I knew that the fiend was pursuing me. I started to run, hoping that I could make one of the side turnings I had previously explored. But it was no use. I felt my left wrist roughly grasped and a voice hissed in my ear, "Come with me. You are what I want."

I wondered if he was going to kill me. After all, I suppose he could easily have done so if he had wanted to. Certainly no one in the café would have taken any steps to prevent him doing so. They were all much too terrified. I went, for I had no choice. My captor then proceeded to explain, though owing to my ignorance of the French language I was unable to follow his meaning at the time, that he was the leader of an apache gang in Paris, and that he was known as White Panther on account of his silent and deadly assault in street robbery. All this he told me with the pride of a nobleman of ancient family proclaiming his lineage.

I supposed that only my admiration could make up for the insult I had delivered to his vanity, and only my praise could revive his self-esteem.

It was with this man then that I went to Paris. Things had taken a strange turn, as you see.

The headquarters of White Panther's gang was a cellar in the heart of the Glacière district, where the police go in pairs by day and not at all by night. At first sight it reminded me somewhat of my native Canning Town, although I am bound to admit that it appeared one degree at least more squalid and much more dangerous. From the station White Panther led me so swiftly and by such a winding route that in spite of the most earnest attention to where we were going (in accordance with the resolution I had recently taken in Bordeaux) I soon lost absolutely all sense of direction. Gradually the alley ways became narrower and more numerous and impossible to remember, until I almost felt that I was in a warren constructed by some animals and not by men at all, rather than in part of a city laid out by human beings. On every side ill-fitting shutters permitted slips of light to escape. These to my heated fancy were like tongues of Hell-fire.

Suddenly White Panther stopped outside a deserted-looking house and knocked in a particular way upon the basement door. We were admitted, and I found myself in a long room with a bar at one end, behind which stood

the fattest man I have ever seen. The floor was scattered
with sawdust. Spittoons were arranged round the edges,
and deal tables dotted about in the middle of the room.
The room was dimly lighted by a couple of hanging oil
lamps. This turned out to be the chief living room of the
gang. It was here that everyone met and where plans
were made. It was also, as you will hear later, the scene
of several fights.

A number of men and women, dressed in the
picturesque apache style, were drinking at the bar. Still
holding my hand, White Panther led me towards them.
The conversation dropped at our approach.

"Hortense," called White Panther.

At this a dark-eyed girl, with beautiful pointed
breasts, stepped forward and looked at us for a moment.
Her face darkened with anger, and before White Panther
could explain who I was, she rushed at me, whipping out
a knife as she came.

It was a sudden rush of jealousy. I do not know what
the White Panther thought was going to happen. Possibly
he only wished for a fight just to see which was the best
of us. If he did, he narrowly missed losing me altogether.

I was unarmed. It was an unpleasant situation. As
she lunged at me I jumped back, and raising my hands,
warded off her blow at the expense of a slit palm. Then
before she could recover her balance I managed to leap
upon her and wrenched the knife from her hand. I could
have killed her, but this was the last thing I wished to
do. All I wanted was to protect myself now and in the
future, and I felt that I must show this as violently as

possible. I therefore flung the knife away and attacked her on equal terms with my bare hands. Unarmed, she was no match for me. Seizing her hair in one hand and her cheek in the other, I flung her on the ground and smacked her face, methodically, with my clenched fists. I blacked both her eyes, I knocked her nose from side to side, causing it to bleed profusely, but without breaking it. I beat her lips against her teeth till her mouth was full of blood. Indeed by the time I had finished with her I should doubt if there was a single square centimetre from hair to chin unbruised. I must say that I was in a frightful passion. I was just administering a few blows to a spot which seemed lighter in colour than the rest when White Panther dragged me by the hair to my feet. In an instant my teeth had met in his wrist just below the coat sleeve.

"*Tigre*," he muttered. With a blow he knocked me staggering across the room. But from that time I was known among the apaches as "The Tiger-Woman."

I now definitely became a member of the gang. There was really nothing else for me to do. Besides, I enjoyed this life of adventure, and I must say that on the whole everybody was very kind to me. Of course there were rather awful moments, some of which I will describe, but being one of them I had to live their life and get money by their methods. If people are shocked by this part of my story, I ask them to recollect what were the circumstances I found myself in when I got stranded alone in a foreign country.

All the men of the band carried knives, which they

used among themselves at the slightest provocation, and there were always being fights as a result.

Among other people I met while I was in Paris was the notorious Mlle Bertrande, who was sentenced a few years ago to a very heavy term of imprisonment. At that time she was a very well-known figure in the underworld.

Among other members of the gang. was a certain apache who was always known as The Strangler. He was called this because of his way of half-choking the people he robbed. With him I had a tremendous battle. It was over his girl, who was a pretty little thing called Rose. She had deliberately kissed one of the other men in order to make him jealous, but as he himself was always being unfaithful to her no one thought very much of this. However, one day while I was helping a girl called Felicienne to do the cooking, I suddenly heard some frightful screams, and rushing into the other room I saw The Strangler with his hands at Rose's throat. No one took much notice, but I was filled with rage, and seizing a bottle, I crashed it over his head. It stunned him for some moments, but Rose, half-fainting as she was, managed to escape. After a few seconds his senses returned and he came at me again, but again I hit him with the bottle, this time across the face. I had won, but I felt sick and upset for days after this happened.

With my childlike appearance, my winning ways, my tantrums, and my innocent smile, I was a perfect example of how appearances can deceive. But I suppose it is human nature never to suspect others of being able to use the same weapons as ourselves. Many are hoisted, as I was, with their own petards. Who would have thought this would lead to so much? In this particular case it was a young Englishman who was the cause of so much trouble. I saw him in a dancing place where I had gone with some of the gang one evening, more or less on the look-out for something of this kind, for you must remember that we lived entirely upon our wits. To judge from his clothes, a Harris tweed coat, light brown in colour, a club tie and grey flannel trousers, an Oxford or Cambridge undergraduate. And to judge from his behaviour he was drunk. He probably had five pounds in his pocket and an unlimited confidence in his knowledge of the world. I had only to offer to show him something to tell his friends about when he got home, something that would convince them that he knew "his Paris," and he was mine.

My deductions from his appearance were entirely correct. He was not a Sûreté agent in disguise, but a genuine undergraduate, and a very simple one at that. Once I had touched his hand and indicated delicately that I might in the privacy of a cab permit him to kiss me, he would have accompanied me to Moscow without further persuasion.

I took my undergraduate back to our headquarters, where he was, to put it bluntly, made drunk, relieved of his money and possessions, driven in another cab to an outlying part of Montmartre, and there left to find his way home—all in accordance with the usual routine. The next day the police raided our cellar.

Luckily we had received warning a few hours in

advance, and escaped arrest by taking refuge in another of our asylums in the neighbourhood. But the members of our gang were furious with me, ascribing their betrayal, rightly as it turned out, to my undergraduate. They demanded that I should produce his body for punishment, and if I failed, The Strangler intimated, without much good will, I would do very well as a substitute.

For ages I searched for that boy without success. I haunted the café where I had met him and all the others the English are known to frequent. After all, it was more than possible that he might have left Paris. It would have been quite a natural thing for him to have done after all he had gone through. But somehow I had a feeling that he had not done this, and that I should be able to save my life by finding him. I searched for him as if my life depended on it—which as a matter of fact it did. At last I found him. I smiled and signalled to him to come over to me, but he would not even look in my direction. I went and spoke to him, but he refused to have anything to do with me. I saw clearly that he realized that I was probably at the bottom of all that had happened when he had been robbed in the cellar. I was not, however, at the end of my resources. There was an apache cab outside which I hailed by means of our secret signal. I then described my intended quarry to the driver, gave instructions that he was if possible to be picked up and driven to our headquarters, and I concealed myself inside the cab. The ruse worked to perfection. Within a quarter of an hour my countryman emerged from the café and hailed a cab. Imagine his astonishment at finding me inside.

Once he was inside I began to tell him that I was not really to blame for all that had happened. I tried to explain, feeling all the time that my very life depended on my success in this case, for I knew the apaches would kill me if I failed this time.

My companion, however, remained quite unmoved by my words. He called to the driver to stop, not suspecting him to be in league with me. The driver, of course, took no notice.

I made desperate efforts to quiet his suspicions. The driver, I said, knew where to go. He was taking us to my room. I could explain everything to him there. He would come, wouldn't he?

We soon arrived at our destination—not, of course, the same place that I had taken him to before. I opened the door and let him pass in before me, locking it after us to cut off his retreat. I then proclaimed to my friends that here was the informer who had revealed our hiding-place to the police.

Some suggested death. This I succeeded in preventing, but it was determined to brand him on the chest, and I was appointed to carry out the sentence. I tried to get out of this, as I felt that I had done enough in the business, and wanted to have nothing more to do with the matter at all. But the leaders of the gang insisted.

I stuck my dagger in the fire and directed two of the men to hold the culprit, while I tore open his shirt and vest. When the dagger was red hot I applied it three times to his left breast, allowing the iron to sink pretty deep each time, thus forming a particular kind of triangle, which was the apache sign. The victim endured the pain without sound or struggle, though his pallor and heavy perspiration testified how sharply he had suffered.

The smell of burning flesh sickened me, but much worse was the expression of utter contempt with which he regarded me just before he fainted. It was really awful. Looking back on it I cannot imagine how I was able to do it, for although I have this violent temper, this was done in cold blood. I suppose it was the knowledge that if I did not do it both of us would die, which would anyway have been worse.

He was immediately bundled into a cab and deposited as before on the outskirts of Montmartre.

So I punished the boy who had outwitted me. But he won in the end, I am compelled to admit. Even now I cannot understand how he remembered where he had been taken. On the way there I do not see how he could have had much opportunity for observing the route, and few people after the ordeal we subjected him to would have had the coolness to keep a record in their mind of our address and the way to it. Yet one of these he must have done. For the next day the police raided us, without, this time, our receiving any notice of their intention. All the men of our gang were arrested and imprisoned, and the remainder of us dispersed. For my part, with the little money I had been able to save, I returned to England.

Such were my adventures in France, and I think it will be admitted that they are strange enough to be worth describing. I will not comment on them. People may think what they like about my behaviour, and I have no doubt that many will disapprove very strongly. If they do I ask them again to remember how I was situated and to try and imagine what they themselves would have done if they had been faced with the same events. How distant those days in France seem to me now, although they are not really so very long ago. Yet now I know that even while these things were going on I was still a child, scarcely understanding their meaning.

CHAPTER IV

GETTING MARRIED

The Café Royal again—Some notable people—The Crabtree
  Club—Bunny—I get engaged—I go to Cornwall to be
  improved—The Rectory—Life in the country—Practical
  jokes—I escape to London—Arthur—Engaged again—A
  surprise marriage.

How different I felt. Yet how unchanged was London!
How delightful it was to have fat, solid half-crowns in
one's purse, to eat marmalade for breakfast and to step
out of the train on to a platform instead of having to climb
down six feet to the ground level. And my friends—how
would they greet me? I wanted to see them all at once
and relate my adventures to them.

I was received with great acclaim in the Endell
Street Club. Everyone pressed round to hear my story.
No one was listened to but me. As you can imagine, I
rather enjoyed this. You see, before I had been to France
I was looked on by everyone more or less as a child, and
although everybody used to talk to me, this was quite
different. I discovered that my adventures had made me
important. I told them of all I had done, and all that had
happened to me, since I embarked for Bordeaux with
Pretty Pet. I told them of my fights with Hortense and
The Strangler and many others that I have forgotten. I

described my friends and associates, White Panther, Evil Eye, Felicienne, Rose and the rest, and I explained in great detail our methods of working. But of the branding of the English undergraduate I made no mention, hating its memory.

Towards the end of my long recital I observed a middle-aged man of pleasant, though not handsome, appearance watching me with attention and admiration. I determined to make his acquaintance.

When I had done, I stood up and cried, "Watch! I will do for you some dances of the apache."

I began to dance, and they stood round in a circle watching me and applauding. I did all the dances I had learnt in Paris, and watched for the effect they would have on people over here.

They were delighted by my dancing, and yet I have never received any real instruction in the art. Dancing is my natural mode of expression. When I dance I am one. My mind, my spirit, my me, are then my body, and my body is all and each of them. I danced and danced, now a flame, now a fish, now a bird, now a flower, now a wind that bends the flower and carries away its scent. I was all nature, a goddess! And all the time I danced for this one man.

And when the desire to dance had gone out of me I sang, still for the same man, whose eyes had expressed admiration for me. Wild songs of the underworld, in my low crooning voice, songs full of pictures, with sinuous rhythms and passion-stirring melodies. As I sang I became in turn the embodiment of hate and desire, anger and despair, jealousy and revenge. I sang many songs until I could sing no more, and then I went and sat on the knee of the man whose acquaintance I desired to make, and put my arms round his neck and asked him to kiss me.

During this period—just before the outbreak of the Great War—the Café Royal was in its heyday as an artistic and Bohemian resort. I took up again my old profession of a model, and with my Parisian record behind me, soon became a person of some consequence. In all that gathering of amusing people I suppose few names became more widely known than that of Betty May.

In addition to the people I have already referred to in an earlier chapter, the frequenters of the Café at this time included William Orpen, who was even then becoming well known for his portraits, Rupert Brooke, that beautiful young poet who was to die in the war, Geoffrey Nelson the painter, Clive Bell the critic, Carlo Norway, to whose guitar I often sang, Horace Brodsky, the Russian poet, Rudolph Vasey, who was intended for a priest and used to give parties which lasted three weeks and who died tragically in a motor accident the other day, Stewart Gray, the famous hunger-striker and leader of the "Back-to-the-Land" movement, Evan Morgan, then a poet but now a rising politician, Ivor Campbell, who was killed in the war, and Flower Ellis. The last three were very fond of me.

Among the models, beside Lilian Shelley, "The Bug" or "The Pocket Edition," as she was often called, and myself, were Euphemia Lamb, a famous John model, Bobby Channing, Lilian Browning, a girl called "The Limpet," who fell in love about once a week, the blonde Jessica, Valda, the ballet dancer, and Eileen, another John model, who was shot by her lover in a fit of jealousy. There was Nancy Cunard, Iris Tree, and poor Marie Beerbohm, who has just died, and I sometimes used to see the stately Sylvia Gough there, surrounded by men who were hopelessly in love with her. Nina Hamnett, the painter, was the only girl I had ever seen then with short hair. She had a lovely boyish figure and she always had her own crowd of friends round her, as she was a very amusing talker and quite one of the most attractive personalities of the Café.

I should also mention Anna Wickham, the poetess. She was always dressed very severely, and had a deep voice that used to frighten me a great deal. One day as I was passing her table she boomed, "Sit here!" I was so surprised that I sat down quietly at once. She began to talk to me about books and writers, subjects I knew nothing at all about in those days, and at last made me go home with her, where she knitted and continued the discussion, or rather the lecture. It was very interesting, but most of the time I was frightened out of my life, so that I am afraid I did not take it all in. Another very interesting woman was Gladys Dillon, that marvellous teacher of dancing, who was sometimes taken for my sister.

There was Nevinson and his pretty fiancée, now his wife. Alvaro Guevara, the Chilean painter, whose portrait of Edith Sitwell hangs in the Tate Gallery. There was Van Leer, then a cotton merchant, who used to give magnificent dinners and who is now one of the most well-known picture dealers in Paris, and that trio of musicians who always used to be about together, Cecil Grey, Van Dieren and Philip Heseltine. There was Tony Schiff, who used to give such good parties, and George Hill, who later ran the Hambone Club.

There was also Odell, that amazing man, with his noble-looking head covered with long dark hair which seemed almost yellow. He had a deadly white face and huge luminous eyes. His hands were long and sensitive. His nails were also very long. He was tall and thin, and always gave the impression of living alone in some garret and doing all his work by candle-light.

There was Jack Coglan, the husband of Happy Fanny Fields, so well known on the music-hall stage, and Ronald Firbank, the novelist, rich, odd, brilliant.

Of course in those days the Café was open all day, and you could arrive there at ten o'clock and have breakfast and read the papers, all of which were provided. You could also get a plate of chips for sixpence, which was very useful if you were hard up. Imagine such a thing in the Café Royal as it is to-day !

And then I must tell you about Judah, the manager of the Café, who was a very important person in all our lives. He really understood people, and it is very sad to think that you can no longer see him there, playing dominoes with some of the retired French journalists who used to go there. He was very useful when we were broke, for he would lend us money on bits of jewellery or anything else we happened to have. Sometimes he would buy things outright, and then you had a time over the bargaining when all dear old Judah's racial instincts came out.

Of course it was not all fun. There was a lovely little model whom we used to call "Bunny," because she had teeth like a rabbit. I believe she used to dope, but she had a crowd of admirers and always seemed to be having a good time. Then she fell in love with a man who used to come to the Café a lot. She concealed from him the fact that she was married already and went through a form of marriage with him. Then it all came out, and the poor child got six months at the Old Bailey. After that she vanished completely from her old haunts and we forgot about her almost entirely. Then she was the central figure of a tragedy. Her dead body was discovered in a flat at Brixton, where she had evidently been murdered. A stocking was tied round her neck and there were marks on her throat. Then a man was arrested. It appeared that he had had a quarrel with her, and after killing her he went out and broke open the till of a little general shop in the neighbourhood. If he had not done this he would probably never have been discovered, as there was nothing else to show that he had been in the neighbourhood. In court he said, "I didn't know anybody could go out so easily." He got five years for manslaughter. There was poor Laura Grey, who took an overdose of veronal in her flat in Jermyn Street. She had a very sad end. She was found on the floor in a walking costume and white blouse, surrounded by empty bottles

[*Basil.*

BETTY MAY

and unopened letters and telegrams. I knew her well, and the night before she was found dead she came over to me in the Café and gave me a book she had promised to lend me. We had a long chat and she seemed quite cheerful. She was tall and slim, with a very fine forehead. At one time she had been a militant suffragette.

I used to have great fun with a man called Richard and a friend of his who is now a very famous doctor. Richard's family had property near Ryde, and in the summer I used to go down and canoe there with them. Once I was left alone there for some days to look after an empty farm, and all the time I lived entirely on lobster and strawberries. And then one day when we were out in a canoe it upset. Richard caught a cold which led to pneumonia, and the poor boy died soon after. It was very sad, and after that his doctor friend would never speak to me. I suppose he thought in some way I must have been responsible.

There was only one change, and that not an important one, in the way of life of our set from the days before I went to Paris. The Cabaret Club had closed down, and its place was taken by the Crabtree. This was such an amusing place that I think I should describe it in further detail for those who have never seen it. It was quite the centre of my life for some time, and many of my most enjoyable memories are of things that happened there.

The Crabtree Club was in Greek Street. It consisted of several rooms furnished with deal tables and chairs. There were no waiters, as we used to get everything for ourselves. There was often not even anyone to take the money for the things. We used to leave it on the counter after we had taken what we wanted. Not only could you get a very good dinner at the Crabtree, but if you preferred it, you could have a meal of bread and cheese and beer, which one could get at any hour of the day or night. There is no place like that now. I cannot think why not, for it is just the sort of thing that everybody wants. But then, things have changed so much since those days that perhaps it would not be such fun as it used to be then. For one thing, everybody used to do *something* at the Crabtree. They danced or played or were amusing in one way or another. There used to be a stage there for small performances of one kind or another which we used to get up.

Hither we all used to come when the Café shut. Sometimes Carlo Norway and I would entertain the company with songs, and Lilian Shelley also used to sing beautifully there. At others we used to stage stupendous rags, in which I always took a leading part. I was rather a grubby little creature in those days, with frizzed-out hair. I really must have looked very odd. And this I remember very vividly. There was a pole from the floor to the ceiling up which many a time I have swarmed to escape the pursuit of someone I had played a prank on. I must, in my calico trousers and red sash, have looked very like a performing monkey. I often used to slide down the banister, and people would catch me at the bottom.

We seldom left the Crabtree until morning, just in time for a bath at somebody's studio who was lucky enough to possess one, and after that breakfast at the Café Royal.

Sleep seemed a waste of time. It seemed, indeed, as if we never slept. Somehow in those days we could do it. I always used to go to my sittings punctually, and yet one had very few hours' sleep a week.

I had gone to the Crabtree Club one night with a girl friend and a man to whom the reader has not yet been introduced, called Dick, a barrister of about thirty-five, who wanted to marry me. At a table nearby sat a handsome young man with staring, expressionless eyes. I had seen him before—I could swear to it—but I had utterly forgotten when and under what circumstances. The thick curly hair, the broad shoulders, the nervous hands—characteristic, as I learnt later, of a drug addict— all these were familiar, but fret and strain as I might, I was unable to place him. Which was all the more distressing since I was very taken with him. I was, however, far too much occupied with the sweetness of home-coming to think much of this. I asked my girl friend if she knew who he was.

"Why," she replied, "I introduced you to him in the Café—Bunny N——. Don't you remember? He's a Cambridge blue!"

The name Bunny brought the whole incident back to me. It took place before I went to Paris. It was very odd that I should have forgotten, for the episode had made rather an impression on me at the time in spite of its unimportance. I suppose it was some sort of instinct for what was going to happen in the future. I was sitting in the Café with this same girl, and being pleased with Bunny's appearance, asked her to bring him over to our table, as I desired to speak to him. She complied, and Bunny sat with us for a time, and behaved, I thought, very charmingly. After a while he got up to return to his own party, and my friend said that if I would excuse her she would go with him for a moment to speak to someone she knew who was a member of it. I leant back and prepared to watch them go, but they were held up by some more people trying to move away, and from a slight backward gesture of his head in my direction I inferred that they were talking about me. I naturally strained my attention to hear what they said. But all I could catch, and enough in all conscience, were four words of his, "What, that old hag?" followed by a laugh.

"Well, do you remember him now?" my friend asked, recalling me to the present.

"Yes, thank you, I remember," I replied rather snappily. Yet for some reason, although I spoke in this way, I had a sort of presentiment that something important was going to happen about this young man. It turned out that I was right.

But what was I to do about him, I wondered! I brooded over this question quite oblivious, I fear, of poor Dick. Should I call him over, or should I go and speak to him? The second idea seemed better on the whole, as our interview would probably be easier to manage without other people being there. But it was some time before I could make up my mind to it. Would it be right, I asked myself, in the circumstances, for me to make the first move? Perhaps he had no wish to get to know me again. Or he might think that I was trying to throw myself at his head. On the other hand, it was quite likely that I was making too much of a chance remark, probably long ago forgotten. A remark, moreover, which I was not really certain had even then been meant for me.

I debated the matter from all these angles, and could not make up my mind but to go over and speak to him.

He stood up, greeted me most politely, and invited me to sit down.

"It was in the Café," I began, smiling very sweetly.

He nodded in agreement, but he lifted his eyebrows as if he really was not very sure about how we had met, assuring me at the same time with a smile (I noticed he had good teeth) that however the acquaintance had been made, he was glad, and would make no bones about admitting it.

"My friend," I went on, indicating her with a slight movement of my left hand, " or I should say our friend," I added, "as you probably know her quite as well as I."

"Of course, I remember now," he broke in. "She brought me over to your table in the Café. Oh, yes! But what have you been doing since? I haven't seen you anywhere."

I gave him a short account of my doings in France, at the conclusion of which he declared himself so thrilled that he must hear more about them.

"We must meet again soon," he said. "What about dinner to-morrow night?"

I saw that now my chance had come. If he had really said it I could now pay him out, and if he had not he would not know what I meant and the whole thing could soon be explained away.

I arose and shook my head, saying: "You couldn't possibly be seen in public with an *old hag*." With which I returned to my own table and devoted myself ostentatiously to Dick, making him very happy. Soon afterwards Bunny left the club.

I was engaged the next night to dine with Dick. But meeting Arthur—the man who had been so attracted to me at the Endell Street Club and the man for whom I had danced—I decided to dine with him instead.

I am afraid this stage of my story may seem rather a muddle as readers may get these three men mixed up, but it is important that I should tell you about them as you will see that eventually all these affairs affected the others a certain amount and therefore are important, as the end of the chapter will show.

Arthur, like Dick, was in love with me to the point of matrimony. He was, however, somehow more impressive. Dick was kind, gentle, unselfish, considerate, and rather boring. Arthur equally kind, but more decisive. One naturally did what *he* wanted. In his company I easily forgot that I had ever been called an old hag.

I became engaged to Arthur over the coffee.

"Two more brandies," he suggested, "to drink ourselves luck in."

"Brandy!" I said. "Waiter!"—he seemed to have forgotten that marriage was a serious business. "Waiter," I called a second time, and when he attended, "a magnum of champagne—and ask my friends over there to come and drink with me."

That magnum was followed by another, which was in its turn succeeded by another and another, and in short by twelve o'clock we had finished I forget how many. Proceeding then to the Crabtree, we held a really uproarious party, lasting till well after daylight.

When I saw Dick the next day, "For goodness sake," I said, "don't speak to me. I'm very ill. Go away."

He had, luckily, enough sense to disregard the last command, and sitting down by my head, easily coaxed me into drinking some brandy and milk, after which I felt better.

I was naturally in a dependent and suggestible mood. I felt small and weak and unhappy and helpless. I wanted to be petted and protected and comforted. He was very nice to me. He held my hand and made me take a little more brandy and milk, and, above all, made no mention of the engagement with him that I had broken.

As a result of his ministrations I soon began to feel quite happy.

Then he began to unfold an astounding plan. How I ever came to listen to it for a moment I am at a loss to account for even to myself. Looking back, I can hardly imagine how he can have thought of it. But it strikes me that if I myself find it difficult to believe, the reader will need no excuse if he finds it impossible, and so perhaps in the interests of my own reputation for truth I should leave out both the plan itself and the whole incident resulting from it. However, I do not intend to do that, and I can only assure you that it was only too true. It was as follows.

Dick suggested that I should go down to the country and live with his parents until I should be trained enough in the ways of society to become his wife. I suppose as a matter of fact it was not really as extraordinary as it seems to be when I look back on it. I was, after all, much younger then, and I do not think he had any idea how difficult I was to manage.

I was sick of London and the life I had been leading. My mind went back to the days when I had attended the village school in Somerset, when I bounded over the fields by day, and slept at nights, and woke up without regrets, and was strong and plump and red-cheeked and sunburnt, and I wondered if I should ever be able to recover that happiness, that health, that beauty, or was it already too late. Then, pat with my thoughts, came Dick's suggestion—my dream come true. His father was rector of a small West Country parish, and I as his fiancée— this seemed to me a detail of no importance—should go and stay with his parents, in order to get accustomed to the manners and customs of the people my life would be spent among when I was married. It was decided.

My first view of Cornwall was when the weather was soft and pleasant. I arrived in the late afternoon of a fine day in September at the little station of L——. On the platform a rather good-looking girl was waiting. She was dressed in very thick tweeds, and she asked me if I was Miss May. I said I was, and she then declared that she was Dick's sister Joyce, and had the governess cart waiting outside. To get to the rectory we had to drive six miles over the moors. I drank in impressions. The sun was beginning to disappear in the west, and its golden rays made the country-side look more lovely than I can describe. Joyce, I observed, knew everyone on the road. This part of the country was not actually moorland, but occasionally one got a sight of moors not far distant. The gorse and heather did not grow to any great height. I asked a great many questions, hoping to get an insight into the country. I wanted to know what crops did they grow mostly. She told me oats. I also questioned her about those buildings with a high chimney, and what looked like heaps of slag. Disused tin mines, I was told. And she went on to say those other things, up the hill there on the left, were not tin mines but granite quarries.

And all the time I was busy collecting impressions and information. I had made up my mind that I would do my best to behave as well as possible and make friends with everyone. I would really try to learn how to be a good wife for Bunny. I was inwardly trying to picture what my life would be like in this unfamiliar place. These day-dreams of mine! I expected that all conversation would be about simple things. The events of the parish of which life was composed would be, to one who like me had moved in a larger world, so small and unimportant as to be a pleasant relief. And the people, the simple old rector with his sherry and his memories of Oxford—so I imagined him—his gentle, grey-haired wife, the schoolmaster, the ladies of the neighbourhood, the rustics. It would be restful to enter into their lives and problems. Of course it was all more vague in my mind than I have written it down here, but although my expectations were in a way unformed, this is more or less what they were like. I had very romantic ideas about country life.

When we arrived at last at the rectory there was standing on the front doorstep to greet me—not the dear old lady clad in cap and shawl that I had looked for— but an extremely tall, slim, middle-aged woman, smartly dressed in a grey tweed coat and skirt, and a suitable country hat, riding rather high on her frizzed-out hair. I was simply terrified.

As I got out of the governess cart she began to talk, and went on in such a way that I could not get a word in. She asked me if I was tired after my journey and told me how delighted she was to see me. The rector would be in soon, she said, and he had asked her to apologize for his absence, it was a straggling parish.

But I would like to see my room probably. She had told the maid to have some hot water ready. They dined at half-past seven, but there would be a cup of tea—tea was always nice after a journey, wasn't it?—waiting for me in the drawing-room and I could tell her all about Dick. They hadn't seen him for nearly six months now. It was strange to think of his being engaged, but she was *so* pleased it was to *such* a nice girl. She went on in this way for some time, and although now I know that she was trying to be kind and nice, I had never met anyone like this before and it only rather took my breath away. I did not know how to keep up a flow of talk to reply properly to all this.

At dinner I met the rector, who was a quiet, grave man, also very tall indeed, who was not a bit like the

clergymen I had read about, who had always been rather
comic curates or else dear old gentlemen. He did not
speak much to anyone, and left everything to his wife. I
felt like a midget in this giant family. She overwhelmed
me afresh, apologizing for every dish and praising it
in the same breath, hoping I should not be dull, and
sketching a terrifying programme of social excitements,
tennis, dancing, riding, bicycling—they were quite up-to-
date. I mustn't be afraid—where I should meet plenty of
nice "young people."

For the next three months my life was a round of
harmless gaiety. I will not try and describe it in detail.
I suppose it is the sort of life that most English girls
lead who live in the country, and it would only sound
very ordinary and rather pleasant to most people. In a
fortnight I knew all their acquaintance. In three weeks I
was bored to death. Breakfast at the rectory was one of
the things that frightened me most. I remember that we
often used to have grilled herrings, and the rector's wife,
who was Scotch, used to impress upon me very severely
that in Scotland only the head of the house actually ate
the herring and the womenfolk and children were only
allowed to smell it and considered themselves very lucky
to be allowed to do this even. Fortunately, however, this
was not Scotland but England, so we all had herring even
though we were only women! After dinner in the evenings
we used to do puzzles. There were two sorts. Ordinary
jigsaws, where you had to piece a big picture together,
or boxes with glass tops, inside which were silver bullets
which had to be rolled into a hole. I really do not know

which kind I disliked most, and it was considered an extraordinary thing that I did not seem content to spend evening after evening doing these puzzles. There was nothing about me that surprised everybody so much as this. They would say, "But you haven't tried *this one* at all, yet!" and produce a puzzle that was exactly the same as the others except that the picture was different, or that you used a little trowel instead of rolling the silver ball about inside a box. They simply could not understand that I preferred to read a book or talk or anything rather than do those wretched puzzles. At the end of the evening there was a glass of hot milk for everyone, and I was always taken to my room and seen almost into bed before I was left alone. I suppose they thought I should probably go out and break up the village if I were allowed to sit up alone. Well, perhaps they were right after all. There were times when I felt I might do anything at any moment.

How different this was from the simplicity I had imagined! There were no peaceful days here, but instead an endless succession of potty little parties, always consisting of the same stupid and self-satisfied people. Every kind of snobbery, self-importance and hypocrisy seemed to go in the village, far more than anything of the kind I had ever come across in London. I myself was not regarded as the interesting person I had expected to be, as someone who had been through experiences they would never encounter, who had seen sides of life that they had only read of in novels—no, to them I was only Dick's fiancée, who had, unfortunately, poor girl, not been properly brought up.

They were, I suppose, kind to me and did their best for me according to their lights. But when I remember the forbearance I continually showed the solemn bores whose conversation I listened to, and the remarks I did not make, I am of the opinion that I really was not so ungrateful as people may think.

I even used to go to lectures on potatoes and that sort of thing to try and keep myself occupied. Practically the only friend I had was the daughter of a neighbouring farmer, with whom I used to go out and drink any amount of cider. We used also to play practical jokes on the people living round, such as tying string across the drive at night in which they got entangled with their bicycles. One rather unkind thing I did while I was in the country was a trick I played on one of the eight sons of a neighbour. He was an ugly and conceited young man who always used to go about saying that I was in love with him. This annoyed me very much, so I played up to him and got his photograph from him as a present. I went into the town and had a lot of reproductions made with sticky backs, and came back and stuck them everywhere I could think of. I put them on gates and trees and on notice boards. In fact absolutely everywhere.

I ran a stall at the Church Jumble Sale and Bazaar. It was hats, but no one bought any because they thought they were too gay for the country. I was very disappointed, as I had taken great trouble with them. There were times, you will easily understand, when I longed to return to my old Bohemian mode of life. London, seen from the country, seemed quite as attractive as the country had seemed from London. I began to say to myself that the Café Royal, not a rectory, was my true home, and I yearned after my long exile to return to it. As time passed I longed more and more for it. But yet I made no plans for escaping, and when I did escape it was done on impulse and without thinking about it beforehand.

As a matter of fact one of the things that really did more than anything else to sicken me with the country was the following episode. The farmer's daughter I have mentioned above had a brother who was in love with me, and we often used to go for walks together. He would usually take his gun with him, as he was very fond of shooting and an extremely good shot. One day, walking across a ploughed field, he stumbled in one of the furrows and fell with his gun under him. The shock of the fall made the gun go off and he was hit in the head. He was a terrible sight lying there covered in blood. I rushed off for help at once, but nothing could be done. This incident thoroughly shocked me. After that I never wanted to go out at all. I hated everything round me. This seemed worse than things that happen in towns. There one is somehow prepared for tragedy, but here in the country it seemed more horrible than I can say. But still I could not bring myself to tell them definitely that I was going away. Besides which I never had any money to speak of, which would have made getting away difficult, and, anyway, it could only be done after a great family scene. I was sent into the town one day to buy some almanacs, together with a few more household articles, for which I was entrusted with a pound. As my bus drew up outside the station I noticed the word "Paddington" on one of the coaches of a train that had just pulled up at the far platform. I leapt off the bus, dashed to the booking office, the sovereign in my hand.

"I want a ticket to London," I panted. "How much is it?"

"All right," replied the booking-clerk, "you've got plenty of time."

I flung down the pound and, without waiting for the change—although, as the booking-clerk said, I had plenty of time—dashed over the bridge, and plumped myself, perspiring, into the nearest carriage.

From Paddington I took a taxi to the Café Royal. The first person I saw there was Dick.

"What on earth are you doing here?" he asked.

"Lend me some money for my taxi," I replied.

He gave me ten shillings. He was naturally very surprised by my sudden appearance, and he began to ask me every kind of question about how I had got to London again. On my return I explained to him over a drink, with great kindness, that the last three months had convinced me that I could never adapt myself to his way of life, and, I added, since I had consented to marry Arthur the night before it was arranged that I should go to the country, that it was to Arthur that I now ought to go.

Arthur was astonished and delighted when I informed him over the telephone of my return to London and my intention of coming to see him immediately.

"I felt sure," he boasted, after kissing me several times, and exclaiming, "Darling, this is wonderful," between each kiss—"I knew somehow, deep down, that you would come back to me"—he kissed me again, playfully, and added, "some day, you little devil."

I made him sit in an easy chair and arranged myself on a cushion at his feet. Then I said, "You had that conviction because I intended you should have it. I possess that power, you know, over those I desire to hold."

He stroked my hair.

It was arranged that we should be married in a week's time.

Preparations for the wedding took up most of the following week. This was all very amusing for me. I love excitement always, and as this was the first time I was getting married I was more thrilled by it, I suppose, than I have been on later occasions when it has happened. The ring was bought, the licence was obtained, and I had a gorgeous time collecting my trousseau.

Though I had been bred in poverty, I knew how to spend money, and Arthur was very liberal.

We dined together every night in the most excellent restaurants. After the theatre we would sup off champagne and caviare and oysters, and all the things I adore. And the rest of the night till it was time to go home would be spent dancing.

On the night preceding the eve of our wedding I had a whim to visit for the last time the Café Royal and my old Bohemian haunts. We accordingly invited some of our friends to dinner in the Café Royal, and went on thence to the Crabtree. At the Crabtree we met Bunny. He had a girl with him, but did not appear to be enjoying himself. When he saw me he smiled. I went over to speak to him.

"I'm going to be married the day after to-morrow," I said.

He said nothing, but looked as if he had received a shock.

"You might at least congratulate me."

"Who to?" he at length asked.

"My fiancé," I replied, "is over there. Come with me and meet him."

He came, leaving the girl where she was. I made him sit next to me, with Arthur on the other side, and gave him, in answer to his inquiries, an account of my stay in the country.

After a while Bunny insisted that I should go with him to the Palm Court, a club which had just opened on the other side of the street. There he confessed that he could not bear the idea of my marrying anyone else but himself. He said that he loved me and that he knew that I loved him too. He brushed aside all that had happened in the country, and promised me that if I did marry him he would make no effort to change the kind of life which I was used to living.

I felt myself weakening. I knew that much of what he said was true, but I could not make up my mind what I ought to do about it.

"But," I objected, "it's too late; all the arrangements

have been made, and besides, you couldn't get a licence in time."

"No, it isn't," he replied, "I can get a licence in twenty-four hours."

I suggested that we should dance.

I was the first to remember that our long absence together would give rise to comment, if not anxiety.

Arthur, at any rate, was clearly annoyed, and he said rather angrily to me on my return, "So you *have* come back. Miss —— and I had almost arranged to console one another."

"It was touch and go," I replied.

But it was more than "touch and go." The thing had happened. I felt myself once more wildly in love with Bunny, and all he had said and what he obviously felt made it impossible for me at that moment to marry anyone else. Perhaps if there had been delay it would not have happened. But there were no difficulties. Everything seemed to be made easy for us.

So my white wedding dress, veil, stockings, flowers, were all carefully laid out, my going-away clothes were packed in a suit-case. I thought that for once I had left nothing to luck. But when I came to dress I could not find my white shoes anywhere, and after frenziedly going through the contents of the suit-case several times, and searching the bedroom diligently, I came to the conclusion that they must already be at King's Cross in one of our trunks. I cannot understand how I came to overlook them. I had remembered everything else down to the last detail.

There was nothing else for it but to borrow a pair, and the smallest I could get (I take size one) were fives.

When we arrived at the Marylebone Registry Office, my agitation made me careless in arranging my huge footwear, and in full view of the official, the bridegroom, the best man, and the few assembled guests and spectators, I lost both my shoes while descending from the taxi. It was a most ridiculous thing to happen, but in a way rather suitable to this strange wedding.

So unnerved was I by this mishap that I could think of nothing else all through the ceremony, and it was only when Bunny and I were actually seated in the taxi, taking us to the wedding breakfast at the Café Royal, that I realized to-day was the very day on which I was to have married *Arthur.* I suppose everyone will agree that I had behaved disgracefully.

CHAPTER V

DRUGS AND DIVORCE

My honeymoon—Cocaine—Scotland—A curious household in London—The outbreak of war—Bunny joins the army—I am left alone in London—Chinese hair-nets—Divorce—A chivalrous Australian—A thrashing—Back to the Café again—I sit to Epstein for "The Savage."

I LEARNT one new thing on my honeymoon—to take drugs. It appeared that my husband was a cocaine sniffer of long standing, and being a student at one of the largest London hospitals was able to get unlimited supplies of the pure stuff. As you probably know, drug takers have a passion for making disciples. Bunny lost no time in introducing me to the habit. In the taxi taking us to King's Cross I noticed my husband take a pinch of something from a beautiful inlaid snuff-box that he always carried about with him. I asked what it was like. He told me the effect was marvellous.

"Is it ordinary snuff?" I asked.

"Try some," he answered, offering me the box.

I gingerly sniffed a little and felt nothing. We continued the journey without saying more about it. That evening, however, just before dinner I thought Bunny looked depressed. I asked him if he had a headache. Instead of replying he took a big pinch from his snuff-box and sniffed it eagerly. At once he became cheerful and animated. This struck me as being very odd indeed. I determined to experiment further. More courageous this time, I took a larger pinch, and sniffed still rather suspiciously but with more conviction. He had not exaggerated, for a feeling of joy came over me and my mind worked with extraordinary activity, in a way that I had never experienced before. I felt entirely different. I seemed in better health, to have more energy, to be more amusing, in fact everything that one would wish to feel like when you wanted to be absolutely at your best.

Compared with cocaine, all other pleasures seemed flat. As soon as we got to Oban we took a room at one of the best hotels and set out to dope ourselves. At first it was wonderful. I shall never forget the incredible deliriums of pleasure and excitement which I got first of all when I began taking drugs. But later we lost all except the one persistent and tyrannical desire for cocaine, kept to it, if that were necessary, by fear of the awful reaction that would follow if the supply were cut off. We ordered no food and gave no sign that we were alive. This naturally aroused the suspicions of the hotel authorities, who, after some days—I have no idea how many—forcibly entered our room, and threw us out.

From Oban we went to Birmingham, and from Birmingham back to London, where, for the next six months, we were members of the extraordinary household presided over by Stewart Gray.

Stewart, I have already informed the reader, was the originator of the "Back-to-the-Land" movement. His

BETTY MAY

ruling passion, which involved him in any number of
scrapes and complications, was an enthusiasm for the
simple life. In order to keep to this ideal he wore a beard
which concealed the absence of a collar, and, though the
conditions of town life made boots a necessity, he escaped
utter perfidy by dispensing with socks and bootlaces. His
house, where we went to live, was a biggish one, situated
in Ormond Terrace. It contained no furniture beyond
the appliances necessary to the simplest existence. Even
the bath had the water permanently cut off owing to
Stewart's high-minded refusal to pay rates.

The other people who had rooms in the house were
mainly homeless artists and models, who came and
went more or less as it suited them. They were an odd
collection. Some of them have since those days made
names for themselves and have perhaps almost forgotten
about what it was like then. Most of them were absolutely
without any money as a rule. The only fixture besides
Stewart himself was an Indian doctor, who made up very
good restoratives for anyone who happened to be feeling
the effects of a thick night.

The colony was divided into households, but the habit
of borrowing resulted in something like what communism
ought to be. The drugs, however, which I was still taking
heavily, were hidden by us, and one pretty model who
was staying there used, I remember, to hide her dresses
under the bed. I remember I used to cook a certain well-
known artist's breakfast there every morning, for which
I was paid sixpence a time.

Stewart alone was inflexible. Even in prison, where

his notions of simple finance frequently landed him, he did not weaken, and starved rather than pander to the social system he disapproved of by partaking of the comparatively simple diet provided for prisoners.

The life of this little colony was broken up by the war. Not, however, before one of its mainstays, the Indian doctor, left us as a consequence of having made his dinner off a couple of poisoned kippers stolen from Lilian Shelley.

Bunny, unlike others, joined the army at once, and was sent to Bisley for training. I followed him there and took a farm house about three miles from the camp, where we used to entertain the officers in the wildest style. Most of them were bachelors, so they were glad to come over and have parties at our house, where they could get good food and comfort. Something different to just sitting in the mess.

I amazed everyone by my personality and behaviour. At first some of the more stodgy did not know what to make of me, and were accordingly stand-offish or positively disagreeable. But by the time Bunny left for France in December I was the darling of the entire camp.

After Bunny's departure I went to the flat he had taken for me in Richmond, and settled down to wait patiently till he came back. For ages I was occupied with sorrow and anxiety, and then as these faded, I grew bored. Richmond is a nice place, but it is a long way from the Café Royal. Really there was nothing to do there at all.

Life quickly fell into the old routine I was used to. A

good many members of our circle remained at home, either because they were unfit, or because they disapproved of fighting, and there was always a supply of officers on leave, anxious to have forty-eight hours of fun, and with plenty of money in their pockets. The return of one of our friends was always celebrated by a grand dinner at the Eiffel Tower or some other well-known restaurant, followed by an all-night party.

I took a job in a hairdresser's and tobacconist's shop in the Buckingham Palace Road. I felt that I ought to do some work that would release a man for the army. My duties consisted of serving behind the counter, selling cigarettes, matches, pipe-cleaners, brushes, combs, hair-nets, etc., and in taking the money for shaves and haircuts. I entered into my new business with enthusiasm, but I feel now that I was not very capable about money—I always asked the customers how much I ought to take and what change they were entitled to, which would have stood in the way of my making a success of trade. As a matter of fact, I am sure it worked, in one way, and I was never cheated. People were usually so amused when they were asked to do this that they would take great trouble to explain a lot of arithmetic to me, none of which, I am afraid, I ever listened to. I do not much regret that my career in that line was brought to an end in the following rather absurd manner.

One day I was getting down a box of hair-nets, when I noticed a label stating that they were manufactured in China. The evening before I had read in the paper that a certain woman had been found suffering from leprosy which she had caught from . . . a Chinese hair-net. I rushed to a mirror . . . had I? . . . Yes, there were three white spots on my forehead. Hatless, in my white overall, I ran out of the shop and got on a bus which happened to be going to Piccadilly (I can't say why I got on to a bus). Never before or since have I experienced the same despair. I warned the other occupants of the bus to keep away from me and refused to let the conductor touch my money for fear of infecting them with my disease. I need hardly tell you that everybody was very surprised and frightened and thought I was mad.

At Piccadilly Circus I jumped from the bus and went to say farewell to my friends and the Café Royal. I announced that I had got leprosy.

"Have a double brandy," someone suggested, but I refused at first. I was amazed that nobody seemed to be in the least afraid of catching this dreadful disease from me. Everyone took it quite calmly.

"Promise you will smash the glass afterwards," I then demanded. "Leprosy is terribly catching." People actually laughed when I said this. I still could not make out why I was not taken seriously.

They agreed to smash the glass, and I drank the brandy down at a gulp. I had another and began to have a small hope that none of the nets I had handled were leprous. There was a chance. I had a third brandy. A distinct chance. But I never went back to the hairdresser's shop.

One night shortly after this it came to me that I must see Bunny again. Leave was rather difficult to obtain just then, but I told Carlo to wire to him that he must come home at once.

I had heard nothing from him. And then suddenly he turned up at the Café Royal, fuming. "What the Hell did you mean by that wire?" he demanded, in a tone I will not tolerate from anyone.

I suppose he had some right to be annoyed and I ought not to have behaved as I did. Anyway, that is neither here nor there. This, at any rate, is what happened.

"I just thought I'd like to see you," I replied carelessly.

"And may I ask where you've been?"

I told him of some of my escapades.

"All right, then," he said. "I shall instruct my solicitor to start divorce proceedings at once."

"Do," I retorted, leaving him. "If you want to do that I will provide you plenty of evidence."

I must confess that during the war I suppose I did not behave myself very well. It was such a hectic time when everybody was trying to crowd what might be the last human pleasure they would ever know into a few hours' leave and no one knew from one day to the next how long they would live. You were rushing about the whole time, and everybody seemed to have money to spend in a way they had never done before. I threw myself into this rather wild gaiety with all the violence of which my very violent nature is capable, and if people blame me for it they should remember that I was not the only one who did so. Besides which the war would have been even more awful than it was if the men on leave had not been able to get a little fun out of life. In a way it all seems a rather confused memory to me. I was always reading in the papers or hearing from other people of the deaths of old friends. It was awful—it seemed sometimes as if everyone one had ever known would be killed. And yet all the time other people were appearing, and one went on dancing and rioting in an effort to forget how dreadful it all was.

To subdue any heartache on Bunny's account I took to doping and drinking more heavily than ever. Already before the war, Bunny and I had been admitted to the circle which included Billie Carleton and Ada Song Ping You, an English girl married to a Chinese, who, the magistrate declared, "acted as the high priestess at these unholy rites," when sentencing her to five months' imprisonment. There was one woman who had a very well furnished flat just off Edgware Road, where she used to give dope parties. All forms of drug-taking used to be indulged in. When I first went there it was opium. There was a lovely girl among the party whom Bunny and I saw home at three o'clock in the afternoon after a party that had lasted from ten o'clock on the previous night. We said good-bye to her when we reached her flat. The next day we read that her body had been fished out of the river near London Bridge.

About this time I met Mrs. Ping You, whom I mentioned above. She was one of the prettiest and most charming women I have ever met. She lived near Russell Square and had a dear little daughter of about nine years old. This was before she married her Chinese husband.

After she married him she went down to Chinatown to live, away in the East End. Ping You had been an opium smoker since the age of eleven and it was from him that Ada learned her knowledge of opium and its methods of cooking.

It was at one of these parties that Billie Carleton turned up. She came straight from the theatre in which she had been appearing, and before long she was in the most sketchy of undergarments and stretched on the piles of cushions, smoking.

The last time I saw Ada Ping You was when she came into the Café Royal in what was more or less Oriental dress. I had not seen her for some time, and went over to where she was sitting. I noticed that all her finger-nails were more than an inch long.

"Why don't you cut your nails?" I said, without thinking much about it.

She drew herself up.

"How dare you!" she said. "It is the fashion in *our* country."

You can see by this how thoroughly she had given herself over to the ways of the East.

Even then I had been taking about one hundred grains—ten is a fatal dose to an unaccustomed person —of cocaine per day, varied occasionally with injections of morphia, and my mind and body had already suffered the inevitable effects. I was a victim to morbid suspicious mania, and frequently tried to commit suicide on the most absurd grounds. Once in a West End restaurant the waiter brought me white coffee instead of black. Immediately I concluded that the whole world was against me, that not only my friends but even my favourite waiter had entered into a conspiracy to prevent my drinking black coffee. In a frightful paroxysm of despair I drew a hat pin and was only prevented from an attempt on my own life by the prompt intervention of my right-hand neighbour. This shows you the sort of state I was in. I might easily have decided to kill myself on some occasion when there was no one there to prevent me from doing so. As it happened I escaped this danger. Another terrible fear I felt was that the buildings under which I passed would fall in upon me, and again, when on waking up after an orgy I could hardly open my mouth, I was convinced that I had got lockjaw. Physically I was in an equally bad state. Severe headaches and that maddening itch of the skin known as the cocaine bug were chronic afflictions whenever I was not under the influence of drugs. On one occasion I nearly died. Walking with my husband and a friend down Lisle Street one night, I fell suddenly to the ground as rigid as death. I lay there without moving. I was not totally unconscious, and I remember thinking to myself how amusing it would be if this were really death. I could see the anxious face of my husband bending over me, and I heard his friend say, "She's gone."

I tried to smile. It was so funny. But my face muscles were set and would not respond. Luckily we were near a chemist, from whom my husband obtained some amyl nitrite. He broke the tube of amyl nitrite into a handkerchief, which he held over my mouth and nose. Asphyxia had already set in, but the stuff brought the blood rushing to my head, and in a few minutes I was revived. But it had been a near thing.

I cannot describe to you what an awful bondage this craving for drugs was. One could never think of anything else. I am not going to be hypocritical about it. Now that I have come out to the other side I am glad to have had the experience. I remember the excitements I got out of all and must admit that I enjoyed them. On the other hand, I must also admit that what one went through did not make them. worth while. I love feeling free more than anything else in the world, and when one is taking drugs seriously one never does feel free. Often I lost my voice entirely. Sometimes I felt so desperate that I used to tear all my clothes to pieces in front of my husband, who was terrified of me when I was in one of my rages. I used to run away, and Bunny would have to make inquiries in the neighbourhood for "a girl who snaps her fingers at everybody."

There is a picture by B. N. Satterthwaite, an old friend of mine, reproduced in this book which shows me in one of my angry moods. I think it has caught something of me when I am about to be violent, and for that reason I mention it now to draw your attention to it.

By the time of my breach with Bunny I had progressed to one hundred and fifty grains—that is about half a gram a day, and I don't remember how much at night—and the severity of the after-effects had increased in proportion. I was in a bad way. Indeed, if I had not chanced to meet a burly and chivalrous Australian, I should certainly not be writing this book. He was absolutely responsible for

BETTY MAY. BY B. N. SATTERTHWAITE

saving my life, and I shall always feel grateful to him for this, if there were no other reasons why I should keep him in my memory.

He was a major in the Australian army, and looked very fine in his uniform. His name was Roy.

"Look here, kid," he remarked the first evening we met, in the direct, masterful way he always spoke in, "you've got to cut the drink and the dope right out from this evening. And what's more, you're going to marry me, so I can see that you do."

This was too good. He had the bronzed complexion, the clear blue eyes accustomed to focusing distant objects, the firm jaw, the gentle voice with a hint of suppressed power in it. In fact, a lot of very attractive qualities. Also he was a hypnotist.

"When's the wedding?" I inquired, 'calling his bluff,' as he would have phrased it.

"You leave that to me."

Well, I had no objection to playing a hand with him. I accepted his invitation to meet him next day for lunch at the Monico, only stipulating that, for modesty's sake, my friend Bobby Charming should accompany me. He approved.

The party took place as arranged, and we talked lightly about our approaching marriage. Before we parted I mentioned that in a certain shop was a pair of beautiful top boots which I had long desired to have. I did not think any more about this stray remark of mine.

The next day, to my surprise, a parcel arrived at my address containing the boots and a note which said:

"You will lunch with me at the Café Royal to-day at one o'clock."

If he could bluff, so could I. I went round to the Café at about half-past twelve and invited all the friends I could find to meet my fiancé at lunch. By the time Roy arrived I had about twenty-five of us assembled drinking cocktails. I introduced Roy to them and explained that 1 had taken the liberty of inviting some friends to lunch with us in honour of our betrothal. The lunch was worthy of the occasion. I ordered all the most expensive dishes on the menu, and champagne. As each course was brought I watched Roy to see if he had had enough, but he never flinched, and paid the bill at the end—goodness knows what it amounted to—like a gentleman.

Baffled again, I was determined to show him that I should be too great a nuisance to make it worth his while to run after me, and so when he asked me what I was going to do that afternoon I replied that as I was going to be married shortly I ought to go and buy some suitable clothes.

"All right," he said, "I'll come with you."

It *was* a shopping expedition. I recklessly ordered garment after garment, each costlier than the last, until I had let him in for at least two hundred pounds. Still he gave no sign of quitting, and asked with only a faintly ironical smile if I was quite sure I had got all I wanted. His composure provoked me.

"Not quite," I said, and indicated to the assistant a coat made of the most aggressively striped material I have ever seen.

"You can't wear that," exclaimed this man of stone, showing agitation for the first time.

"You watch," I triumphantly replied, walking out into the street in it. But this was the only and very slight triumph I had over him. It was he who defeated me all the way through.

He had to return to Aldershot that night—he was a major in the R.A.M.C.—but before going he established me in a furnished flat in Earl's Court, the rent paid three months in advance, where, he said, I could live till we were able to get married. Here I remained for ten days, awaiting his next move, the conviction gradually becoming stronger that he had at last had enough.

Then one day Roy arrived with a day's leave and a special licence.

I told him that I was already married, and that as I had no intention of going to gaol for bigamy the joke had better stop. It had been good fun while it lasted. I thanked him for the good time he had given me, and hoped I should see him again some time at the Café Royal, where I was nearly always to be found. I took a step towards the door.

"Wait a minute, kid," he said; "not so fast. If you're married you'll have to get a divorce—with me as co-respondent."

I had lost. As it happened the divorce was not necessary.

Poor Bunny's death in France did away with the need for waiting till the divorce had gone through, and within a short time I was married to Roy at the Henrietta

Street registry office, where so many romantic weddings have taken place. After the ceremony we celebrated at Simpson's in the Strand.

I took up my abode permanently in the flat in Fawcett Street, where my husband visited me whenever he could get leave, and I promised to give up taking drugs or spirits during his absence.

I did not keep this promise. I could not. I used to come across old friends of mine with whom I had gone to dope parties, and gradually the temptation to enjoy the excitement of drugs and the fact that I was lonely became too much for me and I began to take to drugs again. Roy returned one day to find me recovering from a dope party, which had lasted three days and three nights. He took off his Sam Browne belt and gave me the severest beating with it I have ever had, which aroused me from the coma into which I had fallen. It was dreadful. I shudder even now when I think of it, but it had the right effect. It cured me. When it was over he carried me to bed, and there I lay between life and death for three weeks.

Roy's intervention was my farewell to drug-taking. For three weeks I was so dangerously ill that Roy was granted special leave to look after me. All that time I had to be in a darkened room. Both light and noise were indescribably painful to me. A door opening downstairs sounded like an explosion.

When I was sufficiently recovered to travel, Roy took me down to Hastings, where he was stationed at the time. Here, by strictly limiting and progressively reducing my allowance of cocaine, he eventually assisted me to overcome my craving for it. It took a certain time to do, and there were moments when I felt that I should never be able to give it up, but in time I gradually began to feel more and more able to live without it, and as I was extremely happy with Roy the need for it at last disappeared. I felt that I was free once more.

About two months after my removal from London Roy was transferred to France, and I was left once more alone. For the next two years he, was only able to visit me occasionally, and for very short periods, but, so grateful was I for what he had done for me, and so profound was my respect for his character, that during the whole of that time I never reverted to drug-taking, and remained faithfully in Hastings without paying a single visit to London or the Café Royal.

For no other man I have ever known could I have done as much. Before and since being under Roy's influence I have obeyed no one. Not to disappoint him was the sole and precious ambition of my life, until . . .

There was no need for me to have found them. I was led to them by Fate. Once more I was on the edge of a permanent security. Once more my fate contrived to turn me back. And by a devilish trick, I shall never forget the shock and the anguish of discovering his infidelity—that he of all people should have been deceiving me.

He wrote asking me to send out some gear he had left behind on his last leave, and rummaging among our trunks I came across a bundle of love-letters, tied up neatly with pink ribbon, from a French girl.

We were divorced.

It was in this way then that I found myself back in my old haunts. I was more fit to face the world now, cured as I was of my drug-taking, and by this time I had seen enough of life to feel pretty confident in my powers of looking after myself.

"I thought you were dead," exclaimed the waiter who brought me the first brandy and soda I had tasted for two years.

And indeed I was welcomed back to the Café Royal like one returned from the dead. My old friend, Judah, the manager, the head waiter, and all his staff crowded round me to hear what I had been doing. Parties were given in my honour. London held out its arms to greet me.

And I—was myself again. People I knew and utter strangers accumulated round my table until half the café was talking to me. More and more drinks were ordered. We revelled as though it were our last night on earth. And with every fresh round the toast was always "Betty."

It was some time after these events that another important incident in my life occurred. After describing so many rather dreadful things that have happened to me at one time or another I think I should now tell you something which contrasts very strongly with the adventurous side of my life. It is one of my most pleasant recollections and always will be. After all I had been through it came as a wonderful relief.

Ever since Epstein had first spoken to me ages before

at the Café Royal we had met on and off and he and his wife had always been very kind to me. I always wanted to sit for him, but he always regarded me as a sort of child and did not think me sufficiently developed and interesting to be a suitable model for him. Then one day I met his wife, Peggy, who seems to me to be an absolutely perfect wife for a great sculptor, and she asked me to come round to tea with them the next day at their house in Guilford Street. After tea, to my intense delight, Epstein suddenly said in his deep, mellow voice, "Betty, I think the time has come for you to sit for me." I was delighted. It was in a way such a surprise, though at the same time I had always had a very strong feeling that one of these days I *should* sit for him. So every day I used to arrive at his studio at nine o'clock, and often did not leave until seven or eight, while he worked on the bust that was later to be known to the world as "The Savage." There was something so restful and peaceful about sitting for Epstein after all the goings-on I have described that it was really like a tonic for me. First of all I felt horribly nervous. Epstein made me pose, and then began making various suggestions and alterations, and gazed at me from various distances from beneath his figures. Gradually I became less nervous, and Epstein suddenly said, "Hold that pose for a moment."

I should like to mention that although the bust, when it was shown at the Leicester Galleries, was called "The Savage," to Epstein himself, like all his other work, it was known merely by the name of its model. To him it was simply "Betty." This is a matter of great pride to me. Epstein also did another head of me which endless people have told me looks like the head of Beethoven.

Epstein would stand moulding the clay into shape, and sometimes he would say, " Sing something, Betty. Sing one of your songs," and I would sing " Sigh no more, ladies," or " The Raggle-Taggle Gipsies," or " Bonnie Earl o' Murray," and sometimes Epstein would join in with his great deep voice. On other occasions he would remain silent all through the day, thinking only of his work.

After work he would sometimes take me out to dinner with Peggy. We sometimes went to the Isola Bella in Soho, where he made me taste his famous egg-flip, a most wonderful concoction, which he is very fond of. It was at times such as these that I got to know what a magnificent woman Mrs. Epstein is, and how she understands looking after an artist. She never allows him to be disturbed when he is working. She smooths out everything and the whole household runs on oiled wheels. She knows just when to have a meal ready and when not to bother about it if her husband wants to go on working. What a pity every man of genius cannot have such a wife.

CHAPTER VI

THE MYSTIC

It was soon after this that I met Raoul and we began to go out a lot together. At the time I am thinking of it was past midnight and pouring with heavy, warm rain, as if it were coming down from a shower-bath.

Raoul and I were both in evening dress, without wraps or protection of any kind. We had been dancing at the Harlequin Club, and he had had one of his sudden impulses to go out as we were for a walk in the rain. It was the sort of mad thing he loved doing.

"It's the most glorious sensation in the world," he said to me. He was very clever, and had rather a deep voice and always talked in short, excited bursts. His age was twenty-three, but his complexion was that of a boy of fifteen.

We walked round and round Golden Square.

"The great thing is to abandon yourself," .he explained carefully and seriously. "Revel in wetness." His collar and shirt were by now a slimy pulp. "My collar feels as if it were made of soft velvet. But if I had on a mackintosh every drop that penetrated to my linen would positively sear my soul. It's just a matter of acceptance." Then he branched off on a long description of how he spent a night naked on a moor, in the rain.

I did not listen very closely. I was thinking how extraordinary this all was. The war was over at last and life seemed to have become less hectic and muddled. By this time I was quite well known, and yet here I was on the point of getting married again with little prospect of it being more of a success than it had been in the past.

Who was this impulsive, clear-eyed boy? Why was I walking with him? The sane, sensible explanation was that he had fallen in love with me, and we were shortly to be married. . . . Quite simple.

I had often been told about him by friends of mine from Oxford, where he was regarded as something of a hero because of his roof-climbing and other escapades. I had always heard that he was a great woman-hater and that women bored him so much that he would hardly speak to them even if introduced. In this, at least, he was different to most other admirers I have had, most of whom have held quite different views on this subject. The first time I saw him was in the Harlequin. He jerked back his long fair hair when we were introduced and asked in his very man-of-the-world voice, "May I sit down?" I made room for him.

"So you are a woman-hater?" I said.

"All Antony's love for Cleopatra," he quite seriously replied, "was nothing to my love for you."

That was typical of Raoul, toppling from reality into unreality. He made no answer to my bantering retort, except to whisper tensely, "Can I see you after dinner?" That evening we walked round and round Golden Square as we were doing now, and had done many times since, and he recited poetry to me eagerly without the slightest embarrassment. I was like Francis Thompson's snowflake, he said. But I wondered. There was something of Bunny in Raoul, the same recklessness, the same topsy-turvy sense of proportion. How often had the same thing happened! Roy had left me behind with the same result, and now once more. I thought of Pretty Pet and of White Panther, and my apache days, but, dramatic as they had been, I had never felt so bewildered as now.

"I shall kill myself," Raoul had said—and meant it —"and I shall kill you too, if you won't marry me."

"But you must tell your mother about me," I insisted, for he was such a kid really. And so I was solemnly taken to see his mother. It was all fixed up that we should get married.

The mad dream was materializing—in fact had materialized even to the extent of the engagement ring I was wearing. The ring was made in the shape of a curled snake with tiny rubies for eyes. It had, I believe, some symbolic meaning and was taken from an Egyptian model. Raoul was a keen Egyptologist, and in this favourite study his nature showed itself more conspicuously than anywhere else. A talented scholar— he took a first in history at Oxford, though no one had ever seen him work—he took an expert and scientific pleasure in papyri, inscriptions, etc. But at the same time he had a belief in the occult. He asked me one day to accompany him to the British Museum to see the mummy of the Princess Amen Ra. I consented, and on the way he told me legends of how she had brought death or disaster to all who had, however unwittingly, offended her. "So you must be very careful," he playfully warned me. I protested my ignorance of Egyptian etiquette, but promised to do my best.

I always find mummies rather disappointing. They are impossible to really believe in. I cannot manage to have the proper feelings in their presence. A mummy affects me far less than, say, an old photograph.

"Well," I said to Raoul, "is this the touchy old lady?"

He nodded, then, like the child who reads the Lord's Prayer through backwards just to see if the devil will really appear, I put out my tongue at the Princess Amen Ra. If I had guessed the effect that this piece of silliness would have on Raoul I should never have done it. It never crossed my mind that he really took all these things as seriously as he used to say he did. I thought it was all part of his strange way of talking.

"There now," I said to Raoul, "if I get run over by a bus you'll know who to—" Raoul's face prevented me from finishing my sentence. He was pale and showed every sign of the most intense fear.

"Good God!" he gasped. It was no sham. Without a word he rushed me out of the Museum, took me straight back to where I was staying and told me to wait for him there.

"But where are you going?" I asked.

"Back to the Museum," he answered, still pale, "to pray that she may take her evil spell from you and place it on me."

I saw that he was not joking and that he meant every word of what he said, and I realized that I had really shocked him. This showed me that I must be more careful in the future, but it did not warn me where this belief in the occult would eventually lead both of us. He had taken my doom on himself. He, this boy walking beside me in the rain in his pulpy shirt, and relating how one night returning drunk from the Hypocrites' Club in Oxford he had pushed a policeman's helmet over his eyes—describing how a certain "aesthete" had kept a gang of "hearties" at bay with an umbrella—and telling how a friend of his had been sent down for going away for a weekend with a woman—yet even now he was going under the shadow of a vengeance from ancient Egypt.

We were married, in Oxford, shortly before the end of the summer term. Once again I stood in front of the registrar—this time, however, in my own shoes. Raoul, less experienced than I, was extremely nervous, and at the crisis of the ceremony dropped the ring, which rolled into a corner of the room. One of the witnesses crawled after it and stood dusting his trousers for the rest of the time. Raoul's hand trembled as he slipped the ring on to my finger at the second attempt. I left the office feeling slightly uneasy. Had the dropping of the ring anything to do with the Princess Amen Ra? I knew it was an evil omen. Was my marriage again going to be a failure?

On the day of our marriage a thing happened which, although even at the time it filled me with a certain foreboding, I never imagined would return to me in such circumstances of horror. We were walking through the gardens of St. John's and someone suggested taking a photograph of us both. We stood beneath one of the trees there and he took a snap. When this photograph was printed there was the ghostly form of a slim young man lying just over my husband's head. It was as though the form was asleep or dead, and the arms were raised slightly behind the head, while the head drooped gently to one side. At the time I remember we were amused by this "spook" photograph, but I felt an indescribable feeling of anxiety, even though I laughed at it. Later on in my story you will learn how my fears were justified and how amazing a warning this was of what was to come.

That evening a party of us went to one of the dance halls forbidden to undergraduates. It was rather a sordid place, with a bad floor and a worse band, whose chief allurement must have been the fact that it was forbidden. Rather drunken undergraduates were dancing with cheap-scented girls of the town. Some of them greeted Raoul noisily. However, he was not in the slightest degree embarrassed, and treated them with his usual easy insolence of manner.

We stayed there a bit. It was not very amusing, but there did not seem to be anything else to do in Oxford at this time of night. I was dancing with Raoul, I remember, when at about eleven o'clock the alarm went round that the proctors were coming. There was a rush for the door, and I was left alone. Two undergraduates only had not fled, and they were hiding under a seat in the ladies' cloak-room, protected by the skirts of their partners. The proctors, well up to the trick, and untroubled by modesty, searched that apartment as a matter of course. It was an exciting moment. They were just going when one of the idiotic girls laughed, and the proctors returned and dragged the fugitives ignominiously by the ankles from their concealment.

At last the proctors went away and some of our party returned, but Raoul was not among them.

I was very sick with myself for having suggested coming to the dance. Raoul, with whom I was quite unjustly angry for leaving me, had been against it, because, having got leave to go away for the week-end so as to be able to stay with me on our wedding night, it would have been fatal for him to be discovered in Oxford.

By now the place was closing down. What was I to do? Would Raoul come back for me, or would he expect me to follow him? I was undecided until my hesitation was overcome for me by a certain famous boxer, who had been with us, and now offered to take me back to the hotel where Raoul and I were staying.

I then gave way to one of those strange impulses that I get at times to do something quite unexpected. On this occasion it was nothing very dreadful, but it ended rather unpleasantly and uncomfortably for myself.

I was just about to ring the night bell when I thought it would be fun to walk out to the Trout Inn and see the river and the water meadows by moonlight. I was also not reluctant to punish Raoul for abandoning me at the dance hall.

The scenery around the old Trout Inn was delightful. For a long time I leaned over the bridge looking down into the water, half hypnotized. My soul lived in the water for a time. The water twisted and swirled. I thought of the time in the Café Royal when I had wanted to drown myself, and imagined my own hair rippling like smoke on a still day. And then I imagined that as I lay at the bottom of the river Raoul kissed me, but Raoul remained at the bottom of the river in my place. But who was Raoul? I could not remember.

At last my soul returned to me, and the river and I were ourselves again. I looked out over the flats dotted with trees and I felt a desire to explore. So I crossed the bridge and walked along the bank of the river that was to guide me into the enchanted country. I walked, it seemed, for miles, hatless, and I sang songs, but not aloud. The river bank was unfortunately both sloping and slippery, and I fell right in, head first.

It was very wet and very cold. I was furious with myself for having done such a silly thing. I splashed about for a bit, thinking I was going to be drowned, but it turned out to be fairly shallow, which was lucky.

I dragged myself out with some difficulty, getting very muddy in the process, and returned by the same way as I had come, but in a different mood. Unconscious of everything except my own discomforts, with no imaginations more exciting than of pneumonia or a cold in the head, I slowly trailed back to the hotel, and thus presented myself, a bride, to my third husband.

For a moment Raoul could not recognize the miry apparition that met his eyes. Water dripped from me as I stood there. He asked me what on earth had happened and how I had managed to get like this. Had someone thrown me into the river?

"I thought I'd go for a walk," I explained, "and I fell into the river."

"Good God," he asked, "is this what I've got to get used to?"

I was not going to be reprimanded at this early stage of our relationship, so I said, "And why did you leave me at the dance hall to find my way home alone?"

"The proctors——"

"I suppose you care more about the proctors than about me."

But it was not really a very serious sort of quarrel!

However, it was not only Raoul who had to accustom himself to the new and surprising.

I have referred already to the superstitious side of his character as shown in the matter of the Princess Amen Ra. The following day I was to have more evidence of it, and to be involved to a certain extent myself. A great friend of his, he told me, whom he was very anxious that I should meet, was coming to dinner.

I did not know the name he mentioned and was not

prepared for the rather striking-looking individual who turned up at dinner time.

He was tall and gaunt, with unblinking, almost lidless, eyes, like those of a cat. For some reason or other I felt an immediate repulsion for him. When he held out his hand I pretended not to notice it. I would rather have touched a dead rat or a toad's belly.

He turned out, nevertheless, to be an excellent talker, and I was entertained as well as revolted by him. I got to know him better later on and discovered that he was really a very charming man. But even after I had got to like him I always felt that there was something uncanny about him I am very quick to sense this sort of thing by instinct. The conversation turned to poetry, about which Raoul was enthusiastic—he wrote poetry himself, which was published in various periodicals and in "Oxford Poetry." He was vigorously defending the poetry of, I think it was, Dowson and Lionel Johnson, which his friend had said was sentimental and decadent.

"You're just afraid to admire it," he declared angrily. "You know that nowadays one has to be nice-mannered and impersonal, and you don't want to appear unfashionable. I hate the Georgians. I'm a romantic."

"Is there any living poet you admire?"

Raoul mentioned a certain professor and poet of the occult. I had met him once in 1914, at the Café Royal.

"What's he doing now?" the other asked.

"Haven't you heard?"

"No."

"He's started an Abbey in Sicily."

"Oh, yes."

The subject was dropped.

After a pause, during which he stared at me with embarrassing concentration, the cat-eyed man asked Raoul in a theatrically abstracted, far-away voice, "I wonder what she was in her last incarnation?"

Raoul got up and went into the bedroom. The guest and I uneasily conversed until he returned and solemnly announced,

"I know what she was."

Our guest told him not to say at once. He then asked for some paper and a pencil and said that he would write down what he thought before he heard what Raoul had to say, and then the two theories could be compared. This was done, and he wrote for some minutes. Then he turned to Raoul and asked him what conclusions he had come to as to what I had been.

Raoul said that I had been a witch-doctor in some Eastern country where he had been chieftain of the village. He had loved me, but because of the power I wielded I had refused to give myself to him, and he had decided to kill me. He had therefore set me adrift in an open boat, which was capsized in a storm, and I had died of suffocation from drowning.

This story accorded so well with my queer preoccupation with death by water that my heart gave a jump on hearing it. I had been drowned, else how could I know the sensations so accurately? And was there not something of the witch-doctor in me yet? How otherwise to account for my psychic powers? Undoubtedly I was a witch-doctor still—I shivered—I with my strange, my sometimes baleful influence on men's lives, I with my mop of coarse hair that had fallen about my face or been flung out horizontally as I spun in the dance, I whom Epstein with his deep insight had called "The Savage."

The most extraordinary thing about the whole matter was that Raoul's friend now showed us what he had written on the paper, and to my astonishment it was in its main facts exactly the same as the story my husband had just told. It was a remarkable and rather creepy thing.

I did not see Raoul's friend for some days after this, and when I did I was to be further initiated into the occult. We were having tea in one of the teashops in Oxford, eating, I remember, some Swedish tea cakes, and talking about nothing in particular, when the cat-eyed gentleman, who seemed far less uncanny by daylight and in a crowd, suddenly interrupted our small talk by saying: "You will see me at midnight to-night."

I laughed and answered by quoting the song, "Meet me in dreamland to-night."

We said no more of it, and went on discussing the latest play at the New Theatre, or somebody's cocktail party, or the most recent exploits of the mountaineering club, or whatever it was. Nevertheless, at twelve o'clock that night I awoke with a feeling that there was a third person in the room. Terrified, I opened my eyes, and looked to see. Yes! There he was, standing close to the side of the bed. I woke Raoul.

"Look!" I said, "can you see him?"

"Yes," he replied without surprise. "It's ——. He's sent his body out on to the astral plane."

I afterwards learnt that this man was well known as a psychic and clairvoyant, and as a result of this incident Raoul was very angry with him for frightening me in this way.

We stayed in Oxford for a few days after "Commem," and then returned to London and took a room at the Harlequin, which was run by one of the waiters who had been at the Café Royal. He was a Greek and was always known as Johnny. A very sad thing happened to him a short time later. He was sent to prison for some trifling offence—selling drink after hours or something like that—and, owing to his good behaviour, was let out two days before his time. He came back to his house, which collapsed almost as soon as he had got inside and killed him. If only he had not behaved himself so well in prison the house would have fallen down while he was still in there.

We were very hard up. Raoul had practically no money and had accumulated large debts with tailors and booksellers in Oxford. Nor was he in a position to earn any, since his ambition was to be an Egyptologist, for which, though he showed great aptitude, he had not yet had time for sufficient study. So to enable him to qualify for his chosen profession I took to sitting again. The pound a day that I made was just enough to keep the two of us. Raoul used to go to the British Museum or some other library or museum every day to continue his studies.

Among the books that my husband brought home with him I noticed more than one by the occultist and mystical poet whom Raoul had talked about with such enthusiasm to his weird friend in Oxford. I looked at these with a certain amount of apprehension. I had always heard that their author was reputed to have an uncanny power over young men, and I was jealous of anybody in whom Raoul might take a keener interest than in myself. The event proved that my fears were justified.

One day when we were dining together in the Harlequin a woman friend came over to speak to me.

I introduced her to Raoul, and the conversation worked round to occultism. Learning that he was interested, she said that he ought to meet this man. He leapt at the suggestion.

"I should like to very much," he said. "When could it be arranged?"

"He's staying at my house now," she replied.

I tried to dissuade Raoul by refusing to go myself, but so eager was he to make the acquaintance of his hero that he went without me.

For two days and nights he did not return. I was frightfully worried, as you can imagine. I could not think what had happened to him. I wondered if he had been run over or had some other accident of some kind, and his body was lying unidentified, so that I should perhaps never hear of him again or know what had happened to him. On the night of the third day I was awakened by the sound of someone trying to open my bedroom window. It was Raoul. We were on the third floor in one of those

tall houses in Beak Street, just off Regent Street, and he
had climbed from the street. He was covered with dust
and soot, and his breath reeked of ether. I put him to
bed, where he lay in a doped sleep until the middle of the
following day.

When he awoke I found out that he had spent the
whole time he had been away with the great mystic, and
that he had taken the drug to excite the mystical activities
of his soul.

After my own experience of drug-taking I was
naturally anxious to prevent him getting the habit, and
I succeeded in extracting a promise from him not to take
drugs again. The promise, however, given in a moment of
remorse, could not restrain him from accepting a second
invitation. I protested in vain. He went, and returned
three days later in the same condition as before. I learnt,
too, that all the time I was absent posing he spent with
this man. It was not good enough. I told him plainly that
if he did not give up this practice I should leave him. He
could choose between me and the Mystic. And to help
him to resist the temptation I engaged another room
whose address should not be known. For a time this plan
succeeded—until one day there was a knock at the door.
I opened it, and, to my great surprise, beheld a ponderous
man attired in a Highland kilt, standing in an attitude of
benediction with both hands raised and in one of them a
green wand about five feet in length, round which coiled
a symbolic snake. On one of his very small hands was a
curious ring. I remembered having seen him years before
in 1914. He had dark, glowing, hypnotic eyes and a loose

sallow skin, with very full red lips. He had a massive head, on which was placed a glossy, black curly wig. I discovered afterwards that his head was shaved except for a few strands of hair in front cultivated in a significant form.

"*Do what thou wilt,*" he pronounced in a slightly nasal accent, which made the words sound less impressive than they would otherwise have done, "*do what thou wilt shall be the whole of the law.*"

Like a verger leading a congregation in the responses, my husband intoned in reply, "*Love is the law, love under will.*"

Resisting an impulse to declaim "Macgregor, Macgregor, remember our foemen," I held out my hand to him, to which, bending over it, he pressed his small and red cupid's-bow mouth.

Then he extracted a large bottle of hock from his sporran and announced his intention of remaining to dinner.

This insolence infuriated me. I snatched up my cape and prepared to go out. The Mystic tried to detain me with an imperious gesture of one of his dainty little hands, but I was not awed.

"I will *not* cook dinner for you," I said.

Then the Mystic smiled. "*A time will come,*" he said, "*when you will cook all my meals for me.*" How stupid I thought that remark at the time! How little I guessed that he spoke of a time that was not far off.

I remarked over my shoulder as I went out, "There's plenty of food—you can have mine."

Raoul looked as if I had uttered blasphemy against the Most High.

I knew that the Mystic was looked upon by some as the greatest genius of modern times. One of his many books has been compared to Frazer's "Golden Bough," and as a master of Eastern magic he was unequalled. I mention these things to show that I had good reason to regard him as a dangerous opponent.

I went out into the street in a rage of jealousy. I had been turned out of my own house by this man. He had decisively won the first round. Fear and pride were raging inside me. I dreaded to lose Raoul, and yet I could not humiliate myself either before him or before my rival. Above all, not before my rival.

I therefore stayed out until well after midnight, when I was sure he would be gone, and then looked carefully to see if there were a light burning in our flat before I went in. There was. I waited for half an hour in the shadow of a doorway, fearing any moment to be had up for loitering with felonious intent. Even if I were, I reflected bitterly, Raoul probably wouldn't trouble to bail me out. I was just his drudge now, his drudge and his woman. I thought of the times when we used to walk round Golden Square, and cried. I continued to stand outside.

After an interminable half-hour the light was still there. I could wait no longer. I decided to creep up the stairs and listen outside the door to hear if there were still voices, since it was possible that Raoul had repented and was waiting up for me. This, however, was not so, for just as I emerged from my lurking-place I saw our street door open and the bulky, kilted form of the Mystic step out on to the pavement, where he stood chatting for a few minutes to Raoul. They made another appointment and parted with the utmost cordiality. My heart burst with pity for myself and hatred of the Mystic. Raoul didn't care, nobody cared, what happened to me, I felt. I had better go away quietly, and die. But how could he prefer this man to me!

I allowed time for Raoul to go upstairs and settle down before I followed him. I opened the door timidly. My pride was worn down by what I had been through. If only he would be even kind to me. . . . I crossed over to where he was sitting and fell at his feet, saying only " Raoul."

He looked down at me as if he had not observed my entry, and raising his eyebrows, asked if I had had a good time.

" Oh, Raoul," I said, crying again, " what is it ? " I felt him shrink from me.

" What's what ? "

" You know. You don't like me any more."

" Nonsense."

" Well, why are you angry ? "

" You were extraordinarily rude to my guest."

" Please don't have anything more to do with him," I entreated.

" This is intolerable," he replied, getting up and starting to walk about the room. " You can't dictate who shall be my friends."

" But I don't like him."

"Nor do I like a lot of your friends, but that doesn't prevent my being polite to them when I meet them."

I saw that Raoul was really angry and that it was no good talking to him in this mood or trying to bring him to reason and to see my point of view. At last he said,

"If you like I'll arrange so far as possible to see him when you aren't there. But I insist that if he comes here again you are to be civil to him."

This was not at all what I wanted, so I gave up the argument and tried to win Raoul over by endearments. But he remained angry, and I could get no response from him except a number of sarcastic remarks such as, "He is an extremely intelligent man, and I must have some intelligent conversation even if I *am* married."

At length I gave up my attempt at conciliation, and said that since he no longer cared for me I no longer intended to work for him.

However, our quarrel was not of long duration. We had fallen out because we were in love and we soon made it up for the same reason.

And then came a piece of marvellous good fortune which delighted us both, and which I thought was going to do away with all my difficulties and fears. A well-known titled man whom we had recently met offered Raoul a job at a salary of £1,000 a year. I was in favour of closing with the offer at once, but Raoul would not take it at once on the excuse of completing some research work he was engaged on at the moment, and I agreed not to insist about it. It was arranged that Raoul should take up the appointment in six months' time. Now everything seemed all right. All our troubles were at an end. I was full of excitement at the prospect of having some money and being able to live more comfortably.

I had meanwhile seen nothing of the Mystic for some time, and in the excitement caused by Raoul's new prospects half forgotten about him. But his influence over Raoul remained as strong as ever. They continued seeing one another while I was out at work, and must have then decided, though I was not informed of it till later, that Raoul should join him at Cefalu in Sicily, whither he was about to return, in the capacity of the Mystic's private secretary.

For this purpose money was required. It was as much as we could do to live, much less get to Sicily. Accordingly the Mystic sent word to Raoul that he must visit a certain man whom he described as a great White Magician, but whose business in this instance was nothing more supernatural than to advance enough money for our fares to Sicily. This was the first definite reminder of the Mystic that I had experienced since the night he came to dinner, and my fears awoke all the more vigorous for their rest. Fearful for Raoul, and doubtful of either his ability or his desire not to get further involved with this business, I insisted on accompanying him to the house of the White Magician. At least I could keep an eye on him in this way.

The White Magician turned out to be a pleasant and a cultured man. His wife too appeared a sensible person. They were very kind to us both. I began to feel a little reassured. But even here, even in this sane and comfortable household, the thing made itself felt.

Even here the name of the Mystic was mentioned with reverence, almost with awe. It annoyed me to hear this otherwise normal man referring to the Mystic as if he were something superhuman. And it frightened me too, a little. Was there no escape from him? Should I too become involved?

A few days later I saw him once more in the flesh. I was dining with Raoul in the Harlequin with a party consisting of some other models and one or two friends of Raoul's from Oxford. I think they were Dolores, Chequita, Allan Porter, Bertram Higgins, Arthur Read, and one or two others. We were having a very gay time. Raoul was in excellent form, and evidently much enjoyed hearing new anecdotes about familiar members of his old university. I as always enjoyed the company of undergraduates. In the end we were very hilarious, as were many of the parties at neighbouring tables. Then suddenly I saw in the doorway the figure of the Mystic, dressed as before in a kilt, and holding his green snake wand aloft in one hand.

"*Do what thou wilt, shall be the whole of the law,*" he boomed.

This was greeted with a roar of laughter from everyone in the room except Raoul, who as solemnly replied, "*Love is the law, love under will.*"

A further peal of laughter followed, even louder than the first.

I cannot describe to you how extraordinary a scene it was in this night club seeing a man dressed in these clothes and behaving in this way.

The Mystic moved across to our table, where Raoul immediately invited him to sit down. Mindful of my promise to Raoul, I treated him with all the civility I could manage. The others looked at him in astonishment.

Conversation was stifled by his presence, and I could see he was delighted by the embarrassment he was causing. His eyes rested mesmerically on each of the girls in turn, and from time to time he broke the oppressive silence with a remark usually of the most curious kind. To me alone did he take any pains to be pleasant. He complimented me on my appearance and smirked and smiled in a rather ridiculous manner. Then his eye lighted one of the paintings of me by Kramer that hung just over the fireplace opposite the door. He placed his chair in front of it and sat in silent contemplation—not, I am sure, unconscious of the attention he was attracting—for the space of about five minutes. On his return he declared himself much impressed with the artist's capabilities, so much so in fact that he had decided to commission him to do a full-length picture of himself in all his hieratic robes.

Before he went he fixed me with a meaning stare and said, "It is destined that your path shall cross mine."

I too felt that this was not improbable, and was determined to make every effort in my power to avoid such a thing. But my confidence was beginning to wane. In spite of all my scheming and protests Raoul continued to see this man, and came more and more subdued to his influence. He repeatedly stayed away for days on end, and always returned reeking of ether. The struggle certainly seemed to be going in the Mystic's direction.

BETTY MAY—"THE SPHINX." BY JACOB KRAMER

I did not know what to do. There seemed to be absolutely no way of getting hold of my husband and really persuading him to give up all this sort of thing.

On more than one occasion I had actually fetched Raoul away from the house in Holland Park where the Mystic was staying, and where he had temporarily established a temple of his cult.

Once when I went there on my usual errand I was admitted by the Mystic himself. He did not seem in the least surprised to see me.

"I have been waiting for you," he said. "Come in."

"Oh, yes," I answered jauntily, "is Raoul here?"

His only reply was, "Follow me."

I did, expecting to be conducted to my husband, but instead of doing this he led me upstairs to a bedroom, where he seated himself on a chair and commanded me to kneel at his feet. I laughed in his face. I could not help it. He was furious. Among his followers his word was law, and his person very nearly an object of worship. He lived in a carefully maintained atmosphere of veneration, and here was I, an impertinent little slip of a model, practically putting out my tongue at him. I could see that he was almost as surprised as angry, and pressed home my advantage by pretending to find him even more comical than I really did. At length he stood up and denounced me at the top of his voice. This brought the lady of the house running to see what was the matter. I demanded of her to be taken to my husband. She complied, and I left the Mystic glowering. But my personal triumph was entirely counteracted by Raoul's refusal to accompany me.

" I'll come later," he promised.

This was ominous, as he had never before refused to come away when I went to fetch him.

He returned a day or two later suffering more severely than I had yet known him to from the effect of drugs. It was useless to argue with him. I could only try by the exercise of especial tenderness to regain my partially lost ascendancy over him, and to supplant as far as possible that of the Mystic. In his remorseful state Raoul was an amenable subject. With my own experience of drugging I made a sympathetic nurse, taking him out for walks in the park, and cooking him the most delightful little meals (I am a very clever cook), and striving in every way to interest him in ordinary life and to cure him of his obsession. My efforts met with unexpected success. The Mystic was never mentioned by either of us. Our earlier affection revived. I even persuaded him to take up the position he had been offered at once without waiting until the remainder of the six months had passed. When he had agreed to this, I felt once more that our troubles were at an end. If I could only keep him to his promise I felt that he would become interested in his work and would give up this side of his life. But I was not to have so easy, even if so delayed, a victory. I was preparing our evening meal while Raoul read in the sitting-room, feeling happy about the present and confident for the future—we should be extremely comfortable on £1,000 a year. I even began to plot out how we should spend it—when my attention was called by the sound of something being put heavily down on the kitchen table and by the voice that of all voices I least desired to hear, saying, "Cook that."

"Go to Hell!" I retorted. It was too much. All my hopes were destroyed. I knew Raoul would not be able to resist. Nevertheless I attempted one trial of strength between my own influence over him and the Mystic's. Quickly putting on my cape and hat, I went into the sitting-room, whither the Mystic had returned, and said, untruthfully, to Raoul, "Oh, Raoul—I forgot—we're dining with the Epsteins to-night, so I'm afraid we can't ask the gentleman to stop."

I waited anxiously for his reply. Would he?—no, he couldn't let me down in front of a third person. It was an agonizing moment, a turning-point.

"Nonsense," said Raoul petulantly.

"You must have forgotten," I replied defiantly, and with equal insolence. "I will make your excuses to them and say that you're ill." With that I walked out of the flat, knowing, but not yet admitting to myself, that I was beaten. I went out and had a miserable meal by myself. I now felt there was nothing to be done. It was useless to struggle against fate. I felt that perhaps my foreboding was exaggerated, and yet it was too strong for me to get rid of altogether. I wished desperately that I could win Raoul back.

Raoul now resumed all his old ways, seeing the Mystic every day and often not returning home for several nights on end. One of the people who was very kind to me during this awful period was Euphemia Lamb, and I can never be grateful enough to her for it. I was in despair. As a last resort, when he had been continuously absent for a longer period than ever before, I went to the Epsteins, on whom I could always rely in times of trouble. Epstein, with his bulk and his kindliness, was somehow a reassuring thought, as was his sympathetic and capable wife, Peggy. I went to them and related all that had happened, and asked them to come with me to fetch Raoul away. They were charming. I was soothed and comforted and no longer felt that I was fighting alone against some malignant and intangible force. They told me not to be frightened and promised to accompany me to Holland Park after we had had lunch.

Accordingly, Epstein, Peggy, another model and myself, set off in the early afternoon for the tabernacle, or temporary temple, of the Thelemite cult.

We were shown into a splendid reception room, where, after a dignified interval had elapsed, the High Priest (who was, of course, the Mystic) came in to us, attired in all his robes and jewels of office.

After the greetings were over he squatted on the floor in a position he had learned during his travels in India and Tibet, and delivered a long, and, I am bound to admit, interesting talk on the occult, quoting his own works on the subject, which were numerous. He was certainly an astonishing man. I will try and tell you as much about him as I have been able to discover during the time I have known him and from things I have heard about him since. A great deal of it is uncertain, but the facts seem to be as follows. His origin and early life are obscure, but it seems he had spent many years studying mysticism at first hand in the East, and that he is known to have practised for a time the extremely arduous profession of a fakir. Before and during the war he was in America founding a chain of temples of his cult. The professed aim of the Thelemite creed is to penetrate into the deeper mysteries of creation, and to free the spirit from the trammels of the flesh. As far as I could gather, the method of liberation they adopt is to satiate the senses with the idea of, so to speak, coming out at the other side. It is not difficult to realize that some of the weaker vessels never succeed in emerging, or perhaps do not even wish to do so. Certainly the cult became associated with practices which met with great opposition from the American authorities. The Mystic left America, as he was soon to leave the house he was staying in now.

The present visit was, for me at any rate, very upsetting. When we succeeded at last in breaking into his discourse and making our reason for coming known, Raoul was summoned, and himself, a second time, refused to leave.

My misery at Raoul's refusal was mitigated by the news he brought to me on his return, that the Mystic had actually left for Italy. With that man out of the way, I thought, I still had a chance of rescuing Raoul from his domination. But I was wrong.

For some time we lived happily together as we had done before during the period that Raoul was more or less under my influence, and I had had hopes that I could win him back again. It really looked this time as if things would be all right.

Then one morning among our letters I noticed one with an Italian stamp, addressed to Raoul. I hesitated whether to give it to him or not, and to this day I am sorry that I eventually decided to do so. It was an invitation, or rather a summons, from the Mystic to go out to him in Cefalu. After reading it Raoul announced,

"We are going to Italy."

The blow had fallen. There seemed nothing more to be done. As you can imagine, to go to Sicily was the very last thing I wanted to do. There I knew I should have even less control over Raoul than here.

"You go alone." It was my last card. I watched his face intently, trying to follow the course of his inward struggle. When he spoke I knew I had lost.

"Very well," he agreed, "I go alone."

I have never felt so hopelessly unhappy.

CHAPTER VII

THE ABBEY

We embark for Sicily—Discomforts of the journey—Cefalu—We
    arrive at the Abbey—Life in the Abbey—The razors—Jack
    the Ripper's ties —"We shall sacrifice Sister Sybiline at eight
    o'clock   to-night"—Pentagram—Raoul's   ill-health—The
    sacrifice of the cat—The death of Raoul—Raoul's burial—I
    return to England.

My threat had of course been pure bluff. As soon as I
saw that nothing, not even losing me, would stop Raoul
from going to the Abbey, I promised to accompany him.
He was delighted at this, for although I know he would
have gone without me if I had refused to go, I also knew
that it would be a terrible wrench for him to do this. He
seemed very relieved and did not stop from explaining
to me that all my fears were quite groundless. We began
making arrangements to go at once.

We spent a week on making preparations for the
journey. Lack of money, for Raoul had only secured
just enough from the White Magician for our fares,
made it necessary that we should take very little
luggage with us. I had a hard time selecting what we
should pack and what we should leave behind. At
last everything was ready down to the last of Raoul's
shirts, about which he was very particular, and which,
in an impish moment, I had "twinked" all the colours

of the rainbow. He was very angry when he found out what I had done.

Before leaving, we gave a farewell dinner at the Harlequin. Epstein and Peggy were sitting in one corner, and many others of my friends in different parts of the room.

This had been my life, and these my friends, and I was leaving them.

After we had had our coffee I went over to speak to the Epsteins to say good-bye. It was Epstein who had first spoken to me in the Café Royal, when I was a little girl. At that moment he symbolized for me all the life that I was leaving. I thought of the days I had spent in his studio posing for " The Savage," and of all the times since then that I had resorted to him to help me out of a difficulty. Could he not help me now ? After all, I was still here. No one could force me to go away. So I reflected, knowing, however, all the time that I had to go, that it was fated I should go. And yet I half hoped that he would be able to extricate me from my position. Surely he would be able to suggest some way out that I had not thought of. But even Epstein could only say, " Don't go, Betty. If you do, one of you will never come back again."

That night we left Victoria for Paris.

How can I describe the unhappiness of our journey ? I was weighed down with gloom. And perhaps because of this I remember it as vividly as if it had happened but a week or two ago. Raoul was depressed too, though he would not admit it, and he was helped by being buoyed up with a sort of excitement.

The sky was cloudy and a strong, cold wind was blowing when we arrived at Newhaven. As we got out on to the platform I could just distinguish some way off at the quayside the black bulk of our boat and the sailors and porters scuttling up and down the gangway with luggage on their backs. There were no lights in the station hotel and none in the bleak little town. Only, now and then, one of our fellow passengers (I felt each of them must be the possessor of a guilty secret or the victim of a great misfortune) would light a pipe or a cigarette as he marched up and down the platform to keep warm. Occasionally I caught a whiff of French tobacco, or a scrap of French conversation, which reminded me of my previous adventures across the Channel. The wind smelt of the sea and stung as if it were full of minced ice.

While Raoul and a porter were getting our baggage on board I stared across the shiny rippling water of the harbour at the round black hills on the other side, and followed the line of them round to the narrow harbour mouth where I could just distinguish the solitary winking eye of the lighthouse. Beyond the Channel waves were all crested. We were to have a bad crossing.

Lack of money had compelled us to travel third class all the way, and I found that the quarters below were so crowded, and with such unpleasant people, that in spite of the cold it was better to spend the night on deck. I got hold of a comparatively sheltered place and prepared with the aid of a rug and a little brandy to face the discomforts of the voyage. Raoul preferred to remain below.

The first hour passed slowly enough. The next three seemed endless. As we drew out of the harbour I watched the lighthouse until it dropped out of sight. "One of you will never come back," Epstein had said. Which of us, I wondered, would die? And in what state would the other return?

I felt that our farewell dinner had taken place ages ago, although in fact the sun had not risen since. For a time I was afraid and exhilarated. But gradually cold, hunger, stiffness and fatigue entirely took the place of any other feelings, and we might, for all I cared, find the devil himself on the other side, if only we found also a cup of hot coffee.

At last I found myself in the train for Paris, where I was suffocated instead of frozen. Part of the time I slept. The rest I occupied in looking out of the window. It was November. A weak yellow sun only succeeded at intervals in breaking through the grey cloud banks. The wind had dropped and mist hung around the bare looking orchards. The last time I had seen Normandy had been in spring.

By the time we reached the outer suburbs of Paris my chief emotion was of excitement at the prospect of revisiting old scenes. Those had been astounding days. My life then was a story to be told and to be wondered at. And now the Tiger-Woman was returning to Paris—in tailor-mades and a wedding ring!

On arriving at the Gare du Nord, we walked all the way to Montparnasse to save the few pence it would have cost to have taken a taxi. I do not know how far it

is. It seemed miles and miles and miles. We were worn
out when we at last reached the Latin Quarter and sat
down to a meal. We then had to spend the time until
ten o'clock, when our train left for Rome. Inevitably we
found ourselves at the Rotonde, where, as was likely, we
met several acquaintances. Among them was Lord ——,
who was going to give Raoul a job at £1,000 a year. He
was surprised to see us in Paris, as he imagined Raoul
was studying archaeology in London.

"What on earth are you doing here?" he asked.

Raoul told him that we were going to the abbey of the
Mystic in Cefalu. He was indignant. Getting up, he said
in a freezing manner, "I'm sorry, but in that case I do not
wish to have any further dealings with you."

It was more or less what I had expected. I felt that he
had a certain right to be annoyed after all he had tried to
do to help us and by his kindness in offering Raoul this job.

This incident brought home to me the folly of what we
were doing, and determined me to make one last effort
to frustrate Raoul's design. If only I could persuade him
to spend just one night in Paris our funds would be too
exhausted for us to go on to Italy. I became very gay,
hoping that he would drink a good deal, and in that
state not think very much of putting off our departure
for a day. But alas, Raoul showed a great resolution.
Paris could offer him no temptations to make up for any
unnecessary delay in seeing his hero. My efforts were of
no avail. We arrived at the station in good time for the
train, and Raoul bought the tickets with what was very
nearly our last franc.

For me the excitement of travelling had quite worn off. I no longer had any desire for new scenes. Fear and the longing for security were my only feelings. I had no desire for adventure. There was no joy in it for me as there was for Raoul. For me there were only senseless risks and a senseless throwing away of happiness. Why should I be called upon to make this sacrifice? I railed inwardly at the injustice, and was filled with fierce resentment against Raoul.

The violence of my feelings and the discomfort of the third class carriage combined to prevent my sleeping, and I got out of the train at Modane at 6.30 in an indescribably miserable condition, both of mind and body. Here we were delayed for five or six hours by the Customs, owing to the badness of Raoul's university Italian.

Again it seemed that the journey would go on for ever. We were always having to get out and change trains, or get into other carriages for no apparent reason.

By difficult stages we at length arrived in Sicily. I cannot describe how awful that journey was. Italian peasants spat all over the place in the carriage. I am used to being uncomfortable, but I do not know how I survived it. Extremely hungry, we spent our last money on food, and Raoul announced that he would have to sell my wedding ring to pay our fares from Palermo to Cefalu. We found an English chemist who told us of a place where he thought we could dispose of the ring. We followed his directions and entered an evil-smelling cellar, in which we found a Sicilian who regarded the ring and ourselves with equal suspicion. After long negotiations, conducted mainly by means of gesture, a bargain was struck, and we returned to the station with the money, and bought our tickets, receiving only about the equivalent of one halfpenny in change. So *that,* I thought, is all I am to Raoul. My ring means less to him than the journey from Palermo to Cefalu. I was furious, and desperately humiliated. Very well then, I continued my train of thought, since I am nothing to him in comparison with the Mystic, there can be no place for me at the abbey, and acting upon this conclusion I flung down the suit-case I was carrying and ran out of the station. At first I had no idea of where I was going, and no intention except to get away from Raoul and not to return to the station until the train had gone. At length I became tired, and it occurred to me to go to the British consul and ask to be sent home.

Knowing no Italian, I was unable to ask my way, and spent some hours searching for the consulate, which as a matter of fact I could never succeed in finding. While I paused to try and think, I found I was surrounded by the most terrifying looking Sicilians. They were huge greasy men, and some of them came up and held out money in their hands towards me. One or two even stroked my arm, but I rushed away on my hopeless search. But during this time I experienced what is called a change of heart. I found it more and more difficult to believe that Raoul could possibly find these things more interesting than myself. As my search grew more prolonged and more hopeless, my doubt grew to a certainty. I had judged Raoul too hastily. The ring was, after all, the only saleable property he had with him, and we could not remain in Palermo without money. I ceased to believe he had any intention to slight myself, and gave him the credit of being only temporarily dazzled by the attainments of the Mystic.

I hardly knew what to do. I dared not stand about to try and collect my thoughts, in case I should be attacked by Sicilians. I hardly dared ask any one the way. In any case I did not know where I wanted to go.

I had by now given up all hope of finding the consulate, even if I wished to do so. My only alternative was, therefore, to return to my husband, which I did. I found my way to the station by imitating a train in the manner of children at play, a mode of expression which was luckily understood by the natives. At the station, as in the town, I found no one who could speak English, and had to resort again to dumb-show in order to find my husband. I was first taken to the luggage-room, where, to my relief, was a youth who knew about four words of English. He understood and complied with my request to be conducted to the waiting-room.

There, to my joy and surprise, I found Raoul sitting on the table and unconcernedly swinging his legs as though there had been nothing out of the ordinary in my desertion. I was not so unmoved.

Tears, kisses, confession and forgiveness left me happier than I had been since we started on our journey, and it was in a soft and loving mood that I entrained for Cefalu. For most of the forty-six miles my hand was in Raoul's.

It was nine o'clock and pitch dark when we arrived at

our destination. The village of Cefalu lies between a range of bare rock-strewn hills and the sea. The abbey, which is a white oblong farm-house, looks down on the village from the hills.

On alighting from the train, we made our way towards the village, but chancing to meet a man, Raoul tried his Italian once more. Probably from his accent the man realized that we were English, for he replied in that language. He turned out to be an Italian who had been for some years in America, and later on he was very useful to me.

"Do you want the High Priest?" he asked.

"Damn the High Priest," I told him. "We want to see ——." I mentioned the Mystic by name.

"He is the High Priest," was the amazing reply, and rather than argue the point we said we should like to be directed to him, whereupon he offered to take us there, as otherwise we were likely to get lost, even if we did not fall over a precipice and kill ourselves. It was a long walk up the narrow winding mountain path, and I noticed with apprehension that our guide's account of its dangers was not at all exaggerated. On the way we met various friends of the man who was directing us, and as no one ever seems to have anything to do in Sicily except wander about and talk, we were soon followed by an absolute army of people who helped to escort us on our way, awful looking ruffians most of them.

From time to time the lights of the village came into sight—further away on each occasion, and as we approached the end of our climb we could see a single steady light which we were told was the abbey. It was called the Friendly Light, since its purpose was to guide lost wayfarers thither, where they could always obtain food and shelter, and I thought with a sudden thrill of dread of the lighthouse outside Newhaven harbour, wondering whether I should ever see it again.

At last we came to the abbey. Raoul rapped on the door.

We waited a few moments. The door was flung open. There stood the Mystic in all the glory of his ceremonial robes. He had evidently prepared for our arrival.

He simply said, "*Do what thou wilt shall be the whole of the law!*"

Raoul replied, "*Love is the law, love under will.*" I was silent and angry.

"Enter," said the Mystic to Raoul, as if inviting him only, and before I knew what had happened my husband had disappeared through the door, which was shut in my face. I was alone among these frightful looking Sicilians, who once more (as they had done when I had been left alone previously) crowded round me, chattering and shouting and trying to drag me away with them. I rushed up to the door and began to beat on it. At first nothing happened, and then after a few minutes the Mystic reappeared.

"*Do what thou wilt shall be the whole of the law,*" he repeated.

I only said "Good evening."

He was furious and absolutely quivering with rage.

"If you don't say, '*Love is the law, love under will,*' you will not be allowed into the Abbey," he said. Obviously I could not risk staying outside, so I obeyed and was allowed in.

Once inside, the Mystic disappeared again and I found myself alone with a down-at-heel looking woman whose name I learnt was Shummy. I looked at her and saw she was with child and nearing her time.

"You poor thing," she said to me, "you must be nearly famished. I'll get you some tea." She went out of the room, and I now began to look round to see what my new surroundings were like. They were just as extraordinary as I had expected them to be. I will try to describe them, but I shall have great difficulty in conveying the very curious impression they made on me.

I occupied the interval while she was fetching the tea in taking stock of my surroundings, so far as the dim light of a few candles permitted. The large, bare entrance hall had been fitted up as a temple of the cult. In the centre of the room stood the altar, a seven-sided erection about three feet in height. On it reposed a heavily bound book, surrounded by candles, only lighted on ritual occasions, and purchased, as I learnt later, second-hand from the church at Cefalu (which struck me as being rather comic). Two of the seven sides of the altar were painted yellow, two green and three purple. One of the panels opened and disclosed a sort of cupboard, in which were kept the incense and "cakes of light."

The floor of the temple was of a dark red. Around the altar a circle was marked out in a deeper red, and within the circle was defined a star whose five points touched the circumference. This was painted blue. At one point of the star opposite one of the purple panels stood an impressive carved throne, the throne of the Mystic, or as he called himself, "*The Purple Priest.*" At the remaining four points were placed triangular stools, each about a foot high. In front of the throne stood a sacrificial brazier.

Shummy soon returned with a tray on which were two chipped and ill-assorted cups, a tea-pot with a broken spout, and some milk in an old chianti bottle. I was very grateful for the tea, although it was very nasty. Tea, I afterwards learnt, was very expensive and difficult to get. The milk had been obtained from a goat instead of a cow.

I had another look at Shummy. She was a poor, frightened looking creature, who had the appearance of always expecting, but never thinking to avoid, a blow. I tried to draw her gently into conversation. It puzzled me how she had got to this place. Hers was evidently not a nature for spiritual austerities—or indeed for bodily indulgence. Just a commonplace affectionate little thing, she appeared to me. But if so, how had the Mystic got her into his power? For that he certainly had, I could see plainly. She never gave her whole attention to what I was saying, but started continually and looked towards one of the doors leading out of the hall. Gradually I became infected with her apprehension, until I too was watching that door intently. I was expecting the Mystic, and was prepared for him in any dress or form. But I was not prepared for what actually appeared, and was as temporarily dazed. It was an apparition that would have

startled most people as it startled me, but it was less out
of keeping than Shummy with the cabalistic fittings of
the temple. The door suddenly opened. A tall haggard-
faced woman clothed from neck to heels in a scarlet robe
fastened only at the throat, and with a monkish cowl
hanging down the back, glided slowly towards us. Her
huge dark eyes never left mine. In my overwrought state
I was fascinated by them. I felt as if I were gazing over
a black abyss. I could not move. As she approached us
Shummy said softly, "This is Leah," and thereupon got
up to receive the Mystic, who followed quickly on his
forerunner. Both the other women regarded him with
rapt, devotional ardour.

Raising his right hand, upon a finger of which was
an emerald ring like a cardinal's, he gave his customary
greeting, "*Do what thou wilt shall be the whole of the
law.*"

"*Love is the law, love under will,*" all replied.

"*Do what thou wilt shall be the whole of the law,*"
uttered within sight of the magical pentagram, or five-
pointed star. How odd it sounded.

Then he turned to me. "So you have come to me,"
he said with sardonic playfulness, and I thought a note
of triumph—"to cook, maybe." He had some sense
of dramatic irony. My mind flew back to the moment,
months before, when I had refused to cook his dinner,
and he had said, "*A time will come when you will cook
all my meals.*"

I made no reply, and he went on, "There is a book
here" (indicating with a gesture the volume on the altar)

"containing the laws of the abbey. Everyone who remains beneath this roof must sign it."

I went up to the altar, examined the book, which was bulky, and said to the Mystic, "I shall not sign until I have read it."

"As you please," he replied. "I will give you twenty-four hours, and if you haven't signed it by then——" He shrugged his shoulders, and went out, followed by Leah.

Shummy and another girl called Jane, who had slipped in unnoticed by me, pursued his departing figure with cow-like reverential eyes. I saw that I was a heathen in a nest of fanatics. To disguise my uneasiness from the others and from myself, I said with assumed carelessness, "Come, I'm tired. I want to go to bed."

Shummy showed me to our room.

Physical fatigue made me sleep, but my agitation stopped me from refreshment. Raoul remained with the Mystic talking until about five o'clock in the morning. They had retired to the Mystic's room (called the Koshmar) to do this. I had the most exhausting and fantastic dreams, and it took me some time when I awoke the next morning to realize that my new home was not yet another place of nightmare.

The room I found myself in was oblong in shape, and measured some twelve feet by six by eight. There was no furniture except two chairs. We slept on a mattress on the floor. The absence of any washing things was explained later by the custom of the abbey, which was for washing to be done in public in the courtyard. And I may as well mention now that the abbey contained no

sanitary arrangements of any kind. This was the simple
life with a vengeance.

While lying between sleep and waking, I was
wakened by the sound of a beaten tom-tom, succeeded
by a woman's voice proclaiming, "*Do what thou wilt
shall be the whole of the law.*" And answered by a chorus
in which I could detect the voices of children, "*Love is
the law, love under will.*"

The now familiar words sounded rather beautiful as
I lay watching the golden sun beating down against the
white stone wall opposite.

We gathered that it was time to get up. Raoul, always
something of a dandy, was horrified at the absence of
toilet apparatus.

"Monstrous!" he exclaimed several times, tramping
up and down the room. "How the devil am I expected to
shave without any water? And there isn't even a mirror."

Luckily I had a small mirror in my bag, which I held
up for him while he arranged his collar and tie with
unnecessary precision and carefully parted his fair hair.
But instead of being grateful for the smaller mercy, he
remained thoroughly angry.

"How can I appear at breakfast looking like this?" he
asked. "It's all very well for you, you don't have to shave.
Here, let's have another look in that mirror."

I had dressed myself in worse conditions before, and
was not so much put out, although I too should have
liked to wash away some of the grime collected during
our journey. But I am not sure that the sight of Raoul's
peevishness didn't compensate for any such discomfort.

Meanwhile no one had come near us with any news of breakfast. I, ignorant of the domestic arrangements of an abbey dedicated to these strange beliefs, was uncertain and in favour of waiting. Raoul, however, had apparently no doubts, and strode into the temple, leaving me to follow.

Seen by daylight the temple was even more extraordinary than I had thought. One noticed more acutely the fact that the abbey was a converted farmhouse, and that the ritualistic furniture had an out-of-place, temporary atmosphere about it. It felt rather as if one had strayed into a theatre where one had seen a play the night before to find the scenery for the last act still erected the next morning. I also observed, what had escaped my previous notice, that the place contained a considerable library, which Raoul was now eagerly examining. They were nearly all books on magic and other occult subjects, and among others were all the publications of the Mystic himself.

We were interrupted by the entrance of Shummy, who requested us to come to breakfast. Following her into another room, we found the rest of the inhabitants of the abbey—with the exception of the Mystic himself and Leah—already assembled round a bare deal table, drinking coffee, eating long loaves of Sicilian bread and a kind of cream-cheese made from goat's milk.

Here I saw the children whose voices I had heard earlier in the morning. They were two little boys about four years old, called Dionysius and Hermes, and a little girl of two-and-a-half called Lulu. They were delightful children, healthy and well-fed, and with no appearance of being oppressed by their unconventional surroundings. It quite cheered me up to see them here, and as happy as this.

The goat's-milk cheese had a queer but not unpleasant flavour, quite unlike anything I had tasted before. I did not know then, however, that this cheese was one of the staple dishes of the abbey, and that in about two months' time I should find it so utterly nauseating that starvation would be preferable to eating it. However, the coffee was delicious. Some of the best I have ever tasted.

During the meal nobody spoke, and on inquiring the reason for this, I was taken into the temple, where the orders for the day were posted on a notice board. These always included silence for the earlier part of the day, and sometimes for the entire twenty-four hours. And there were various other ordinances to be observed.

After breakfast I took the children for a walk, and Raoul occupied himself in the library, which, he told me, was an excellent one, containing a unique collection of books on the occult in addition to all the published writings of the Mystic himself. The children, I found, were not at all shy, and quite ready to talk. I questioned them about the Mystic, and found that they had no awe of him beyond what all children have for persons in a position to punish them. They referred to him, familiarly, as "Old Beast," an endearing form of "*The Beast* 666," which was one of the many mysterious titles that he delighted to call himself by.

On our return I found the Mystic, who as a rule did not

emerge from his privacy before five o'clock, awaiting me. He gave a slow smile. He remarked, "You will be 'Sister Sibyline,' and in future you will take over the complete household duties, as Shummy is about to have a child. To-night you will attend Pentagram at eight o'clock." (Pentagram was the principal service of the day.)

"I shall not be at Pentagram," I replied, "either to-night or any other night."

He met my defiance with confident assurance.

"We shall see," he said meaningly, and stalked away.

I soon settled down into the routine of the abbey, although my relations with the Mystic remained almost those of open warfare. He took pleasure in appointing me to the most humiliating tasks he could think of, and I took an almost equal pleasure in disobeying him and in wounding his vanity whenever possible. I was rather grateful than otherwise for the necessity of getting up before the other members of the abbey, since I was thus enabled to perform my toilet in privacy—or so I thought, until one day when completely naked at my ablutions, I looked up to see the grinning face of the Mystic regarding me. Neither of us spoke.

Soon after our arrival the Mystic presented both Raoul and myself with razors, and told us that whenever any member of the abbey used the word "I" they must as a penance gash themselves with the razor. He only was allowed to say "I"—everybody else had to say "one." I need hardly tell you that I did nothing of the sort. I spoke exactly as I should wherever I was. I believe I threw the razor away. But poor Raoul, who took the whole thing with deadly seriousness, could not prevent himself from constantly saying "I," and he was so conscientious that he always wounded himself as a punishment, until his body was covered with cuts. This was undoubtedly one of the things that undermined his health in the first place.

All the men in the abbey had to shave off all their hair except for the one little symbolic curl in front. All the women had to dye their hair red every six months, and then black again. They also had to keep it cut fairly short.

Not only this, but everyone was supposed to keep a magical diary. The Mystic said to Raoul, "You must enter everything in it, you understand—everything. Even to your most innermost and sacred thoughts. And always what you say must be true."

It was a fact that everyone kept a diary, and they were left about open for anyone to read who cared to take the trouble to do so. I read some of the diaries that had been kept in the past. They were amazing documents. There were terrible things inside them. Some of them were attacks on the Mystic. "Write what you please, write exactly what you feel and think, but let it be true," he used to say. He had a huge collection of these diaries, which must be documents of quite extraordinary interest. And so life went on on these lines.

It was my duty to do all the shopping and cooking, as well as to supervise the children when they were not doing physical exercises with Raoul. Our fare, as you have probably inferred from our breakfast menu, was of the simplest. Eternal goat's-milk cheese, bread, tea,

coffee and meat, when we had it, killed on the same day
and unbelievably tough. The wine alone was good, as the
Mystic was a great connoisseur of it. I had some of the
best wine at the abbey that I had ever tasted.

We had only three meals a day. Breakfast at about
nine, dinner at one and tea at half-past five. Everybody
had to be present on these occasions, as for Pentagram
in the evening, but apart from them, and from whatever
duties they had to perform (Leah and Jane, for instance,
acted as the Mystic's secretaries and did all his typing,
as he was always working and carried on a huge
correspondence, sending letters all over the world), they
could spend their time as they liked. The Mystic as a rule
did not appear until tea time. He worked at his occult
writings most of the night and slept until one o'clock,
when he took his dinner in Koshmar, as his private room
was called, with Leah.

I used to take great pains in the preparation of these
meals, but I do not think I can quite explain why. It was no
doubt partly pride. Although not on terms of friendship
with the Mystic, I was aware that my independence had
exacted from him a certain measure of respect, which I
valued dearly, and consequently I was careful never to
appear at a disadvantage before him. And he, I think,
had something of the same feeling for me. For instance,
I was always the person he selected to go rock-climbing
with him. Despite his bulk, he was an excellent climber,
cautious and yet daring, and of surprising agility. On
these expeditions a tacit armistice was always respected
between us, and he proved himself as good a teacher

as he was an exponent of the art. Infinitely patient, he succeeded in inspiring me with a confidence I have never felt with anyone else, even with my husband. "Remember," he always warned me as we set out, "it is I who will get hurt first."

But these interludes had no lessening effect on our enmity within the abbey. As I have said, the Mystic usually made his first public appearance at tea time.

At meals he never used a knife or fork. He broke the food up with his fingers, but it was my duty to hold the towel and basin in which he did his ceremonial washing before and after eating. One day I purposely poured the water all over his head. He simply went on sitting there as if nothing had happened, and I went on with the meal without offering any explanation. Neither of us ever referred to the incident again. This sort of episode was not uncommon in the abbey.

I cannot describe how extraordinary it looked when we used to sit at deal tables in this bare room with only the roughest furniture in it, some wearing the magnificent robes I have described. It was too odd for words. However, this was our period of rest from the severe strain of mystical contemplation. But the conversation even then was of a solemn nature—laughter was never heard in the abbey—and more often than not consisted of a monologue delivered by the Mystic. At other times he would devote his whole attention to myself, in an attempt to put me at a disadvantage before my husband and the rest. However, I refused to be drawn or to give any sign of embarrassment in spite of the fact that—as he knew well enough—the gross things he used to say caused me acute discomfort.

On one occasion only did he really get the better of me. We were just about to begin our tea when the Mystic got up, walked over to the brazier, and taking up one of the sacrificial knives, turned to the other members of the abbey and announced in a casual tone, "We shall sacrifice Sister Sibyline at eight o'clock to-night."

For a moment I thought I must have mistaken his meaning. But his attitude—testing the edge of the knife with his thumb—and his expression convinced me that I had not mistaken his intention.

"You will be ready, Sister Sibyline," he commanded.

I was amazed. I was not conscious of having done anything particularly bad to merit this, but, as you can well imagine, one's nerves were never in a very strong state at the abbey, and I always had a sort of lurking fear that something of this kind might happen.

I looked round at the others, expecting them to give some indication, if not of sympathy, at least of surprise, at the prospect of a human sacrifice. But no one, not even Raoul, showed the slightest emotion, remaining as unmoved as if the Mystic had said there would be chicken for lunch to-morrow. It was apparently a normal part of the Thelemite ritual.

"So you really mean to kill me?" I asked the Mystic, not yet convinced that he would dare to do so.

He nodded gravely.

"You are an evil spirit," he told me. "You cannot be allowed to remain in the abbey to break every one of its

BETTY MAY

rules in violation of the oath you took when signing the book."

I had signed the book as I had come to the abbey, to be near Raoul. Surely, I thought, he cannot allow me to be butchered for having loved him too well, and to the exclusion of my own safety. Surely in becoming a devotee of this cult he has not entirely ceased to be a human being! I turned to him in mute appeal. His eyes were as impassive as those of the rest.

I was doomed, unless I could escape, which was not easy without money and in a strange country. All I could do was to get out of the abbey before the time of the sacrifice, and thereafter to make my way as best I could to Palermo and the British consul.

I felt pretty hopeless at this prospect, as I had some experience of what it felt like to be alone and penniless in Sicily, and also I knew the difficulty I should have in trying to find the consul, but I was too frightened for this to prevent me from taking the steps I did.

I slipped out of the abbey and hid in the hills until after midnight. I wandered about a bit there, feeling more and more wretched. Then, led by some impulse that I am unable to account for, I crept back to the abbey and past the lighted window of the Mystic's study to the window of the room where I knew Raoul was sleeping. I stood outside for a few minutes, without any plan in my head. . . . And the next thing I was aware of was that the hand I had put through the window had been seized and a voice—my husband's—was saying, "You silly girl—of course it wasn't meant. Where on earth have you been?"

I must tell you how one day I was going through one of the rooms in the abbey when I nearly fell over a small chest that was lying in the middle of it. I opened it and saw inside a number of men's ties. I pulled some of them out, and then dropped them, for they were stiff and stained with something. For the moment I thought it must be blood. Later I found the Mystic and asked him about the ties. He was in one of his kindly moods. "Sit down," he said, "and I will tell you about them." He then went on to say that these were the relics of one of the most mysterious series of murders that the world had ever known. They had belonged to "Jack the Ripper"!

" 'Jack the Ripper' was before your time," he went on. "But I knew him. I knew him personally, and know where he is to-day. He gave me those ties. 'Jack the Ripper' was a magician. He was one of the cleverest ever known and his crimes were the outcome of his magical studies. The crimes were always of the same nature, and they were obviously carried out by a surgeon of extreme skill. 'Jack the Ripper' was a well-known surgeon of his day. Whenever he was going to commit a new crime he put on a new tie. Those are his ties, every one of which was steeped in the blood of his victims. Many theories have been advanced to explain how he managed to escape discovery. But 'Jack the Ripper' was not only a consummate artist in the perpetration of his crimes. He had attained the highest powers of magic and could make himself invisible. The ties that you found were those he gave to me, the only relics of the most amazing murders in the history of the world."

That is what the Mystic told me. I do not suggest that he did not say it only to frighten me. Quite possibly he did. But still it seems to me an extraordinary story which is certainly of interest. I have seen too many peculiar things happen to refuse to believe even anything so unlikely as this.

After tea the Mystic would retire again for about an hour's meditation before Pentagram. I have never taken part in this ritual, though I have often watched it. The ceremony opened with the solemn entrance of the Mystic clad in the gorgeous robes of a Grand Master of the order of Freemasons. After he had seated himself on the throne before the brazier with the charcoal fire, around which hung the sacrificial knives and swords, the other members of the cult took their places on the triangular stools at the points of the star. They were dressed as a rule in robes like those in which I first saw Leah, with the cowls drawn down over their faces, and only their eyes visible through the narrow eye-slits. Clouds of incense hung about the room everywhere. When all were assembled, the Mystic rose from his seat, and taking one of the swords from the side of the brazier, held it pointing towards the altar while he intoned an invocation in a language with which I was not familiar. From hearing it every day, however, the sounds remain fixed in my memory.

> "*Artay I was Malcooth—Fegabular,*
> *Vegadura, ee-ar-la—ah moon.*"

The last was a high-pitched note in contrast with

the rest of the chant. Following this, he walked over to Raoul, rested the point of the sword on his forehead, and uttered a further rigmarole, finishing up with a loud shriek of "Adonis," which was the name by which my husband was known in the abbey. Then he went through the identical performance in front of Leah, except that to begin with he stood silently in front of her for a full minute, breathing deeply the while—breathing in the soul of his priestess, as Raoul explained it to me afterwards.

These preliminary invocations done, the Mystic proceeded to execute a variety of ecstatic dances. This was both impressive and ludicrous. He lashed himself into an absolute frenzy, brandishing his sword, and dancing and leaping about in the magic circle. His eyes blazed. The words he chanted had a compelling monotonous and exotic rhythm, and his eyes were alight with fanatical enthusiasm. Every Friday night there was a special invocation to Pan, in which, as is shown by the hymn for these occasions, the doctrine of the cult became manifest. It was written in English, and I will quote the first few lines,

> "*Thrill with lissom lust of the light,*
>   *O Man, my Man ;*
> *Come careening out of the night*
>   *To me, to me ;*
> *Come with Apollo in bridal dress——*"

The rest can hardly be reproduced here.

The children had their own Pentagram at five o'clock

before going to bed at six. They took this very seriously and performed the whole service themselves without any help from the others. Even little Lulu seemed quite as solemn about it as any of the grown-up people. It was one of the most extraordinary sights I have ever seen.

After we had been at the abbey for some six or eight weeks—I forget which—Raoul's health began to give me some anxiety. An extraordinary lassitude took the place of his previous high spirits. He no longer had the energy to take charge of the children for their daily physical exercises, and sat about all day in the main hall pretending to read. I hoped at first that his condition was the result of some psychological stress arising out of his mystical activities. But increasing weakness showed that he was suffering from something more physical than mere morbidity. The Mystic, who had a great affection for Raoul, was also perturbed, and decided to cast his horoscope. Although I did not put any great trust in this, I listened to the Mystic's announcement of the conclusions of his investigations with dread.

"There is," he said, "a great depression over you. A very gloomy depression. It looks as though you might die on the sixteenth of February at four o'clock."

I caught my breath, and he went on. "But you are young, and maybe you will pull through."

I had two explanations of Raoul's illness, neither of which, as it happened, turned out to be correct. The first was drugs. As I have said before, drugs are often used by occultists with the object of intensifying their mystical experiences, and in particular to enable them to separate soul from body and "go out on to the astral plane." Large supplies of drugs were always available in Koshmar for anybody who wished to make use of them. (I ought to say here that it was the rule of the abbey that no door should ever be locked.) Opium, hasheesh, cocaine, heroin, morphia, veronal, were all openly displayed. Raoul, on the Mystic's advice, and entirely against mine, had been taking a good deal of hasheesh, and this I still believe, though not the immediate cause of his illness, had done much to render him prone to infection.

Although all these drugs were left about, there was never anything in the nature of drug orgies that I had seen in England. Only once, on a sudden impulse, one of the women took an overdose of hasheesh. It was while Pentagram was in progress, and she crawled into my room, writhing with pain. I went straight to the Mystic, who was standing with his sword held aloft in both hands, uttering an incantation. I told him what had happened. He gazed at me with unseeing eyes, saying, "It does not matter. Go back to her." He came about two hours later and scolded the wretched woman for having broken faith with him and with herself. "You may have your drugs," he said, "you may have as much as necessary. But they are for you to use to further your spiritual self. But you have abused them." He went on in this way for some time, and every moment I thought the woman would die. Then he turned to me and ordered me to make some black coffee. A few minutes after the woman had taken it she became herself again.

My second theory about Raoul was that he had been

poisoned in another manner. It happened in this way. In the Thelemite cult cats are regarded as evil spirits. Nevertheless there were two, Mischette and Mischu, that used to visit the abbey regularly for surreptitious food given to them by myself. For a long time they continued undiscovered, until one day at tea the Mystic suddenly said, "There's an evil spirit in the room."

He looked about for a few seconds. A moment later he reached under the table and dragged out a large sandy cat, squirming, spitting, biting and scratching, which I recognized as Mischette. She succeeded in scratching his arm severely before he flung her on the ground. Then Mischette fled from the temple, and the Mystic retired to Koshmar to put some iodine on his wounded arm. On his return he commanded, "That cat must be sacrificed within three days." Raoul was appointed to perform the sacrifice.

Leading from the temple was a little scullery where I used to do some of my cooking and the washing up. It had a row of bars, and in between these and the window Mischette often used to sit. This used to happen even after the incident I have just described, and more than once I took the cat and carried her a long way from the abbey and drove her away, so that she might escape being sacrificed. But she always used to return and sit in the same place, so that at last I decided that it was no good trying to help her any more. Then suddenly the Mystic came into the scullery. At first Mischette jumped up as if to escape. The Mystic held up his wand and made the sign of the Pentagram. "You will not move till the hour of sacrifice," he said to the cat. The animal stiffened and became as if petrified. And then her eyes got that red look which animals get when they are really frightened. The next morning I got up early and once more carried the cat, which allowed me to touch her, some way off to the rocks. Within an hour Mischette was back again in the same place. I threw her food, but she would not eat it. There she remained for three days.

A few hours before the ceremony was to take place, Raoul was ordered to capture the cat, put her in a sack and deposit her in Koshmar. This he did, although he was the gentlest of men who would not have hurt a fly in the ordinary course of events.

Everybody took their accustomed position, except that for this occasion Raoul, as he was to be the executioner, changed places with the Mystic. The cat was brought out and placed, still in the sack, on the altar. The opening of the rite was the same as the Pentagram, which I have already described. The air was thick with incense. Raoul recited the invocation, and walked with upraised sword towards Leah and the others and placed its point on their brows while he uttered the usual formula. I sat outside the magic circle and watched the gruesome performance.

Presently, when much of the ceremony had been gone through, I saw Raoul take a kukri (Gurkha knife) from its place by the brazier and approach the altar, on which was the squirming sack. He untied it, drew forth the struggling and terrified Mischette by the scruff of the neck, and held her with his left hand at arm's-length above his head. In his right he held the kukri with its point towards the brazier. The Mystic stilled Mischette's struggles by applying a dab of ether to her nose. All was now ready for the sacrificial invocation, which Raoul had written specially for the occasion, and which he now had to recite in the fatiguing posture that I have described.

It was a long invocation, and before it was half done I could see his left arm quiver with the strain. As he approached the point where the killing was to take place Leah stepped down from her triangular stool, and taking a bowl from the altar, held it underneath Mischette to catch the blood, none of which is supposed to be lost. At last the moment had arrived. I saw him lift back the kukri, and then closed my eyes till it should be over. The sound of low exclamations caused me to open them again, and I saw a horrible sight. My husband, unused to wielding such an awkward weapon as the kukri, had not struck truly, with the result that he had only partially cut through the neck of the cat, which had escaped from his nerveless hands and was darting about the floor of the abbey, spitting and foaming at the mouth, and blood issuing from the gash in its neck in huge spurts. I was splashed where I sat in the shadow outside the magic circle, and a ghastly nausea came over me. Next I saw the Mystic approaching my husband with the bleeding beast in his hand. The whole business had to be performed again. I was almost as sorry for Raoul as for Mischette. Indeed I hardly believed that he would be able to play his part, he trembled so. Even Leah, who must have been more inured than he to such scenes, could not hold the bowl steady. But with a supreme effort he held out, and when the moment came made no mistake at his second attempt to kill the cat, whose head was nearly severed by the blow. Then swaying slightly, he laid the carcass on the altar. This done, his resources were exhausted, and the Mystic had to take over the conducting of the ceremony.

Having concluded the invocation, he took the bowl containing the blood, uttered some consecratory formula over it and handed it to Leah, who was standing by. Together they approached Raoul. The Mystic then flung back the cowl from Raoul's face, and dipping a finger in the blood, traced the sign of the Pentagram on his white, glistening forehead, and so to all the others, himself last.

The final rite, the most disgusting of all, now alone remained to be performed. It makes me sick even now to think of it. The Mystic took a small silver cup, into which he scooped some of the blood from the bowl and handed it to my husband, who drained it to the dregs.

For a time I was convinced that Raoul had been poisoned by the blood of Mischette. But when he got steadily worse and a doctor was summoned I found out that he was suffering from enteric, a not uncommon disease in those parts. It was then that I remembered how he had almost certainly caught this disease. One day the Mystic had told Raoul and me to go off for an expedition together. He was in one of his kindly moods and he said Raoul needed some relaxation. He suggested that we should go to a marvellous monastery about thirteen miles off, where the monks would entertain us with food. But he warned us of one thing, which was on no account to touch any water.

We were both delighted. We started off. It was one of the most wonderful days I have seen. We went to the monastery, where the monks gave us bread and soup and showed us all over it. On the way back the heat was appalling. We were both so thirsty that we did not know what to do. Suddenly we came to a mountain spring, bubbling up out of the ground.

It was an awful temptation. I do not think that at that time either of us realized how important it was not to touch the water. Although the Mystic had done his best to impress on us the dangers of drinking, the spring looked so cool and fresh and pure that Raoul could not resist. He knelt down and drank, but in spite of my thirst I managed to restrain myself, though with great difficulty. I suppose I saved my own life. Anyway, I am certain that this is how Raoul caught the disease. He was at once given the right treatment, but no improvement was effected, and he sank fast.

At this juncture I was expelled from the abbey for disobedience to one of the Mystic's most arbitrary and unreasonable commands. Every fortnight I had been accustomed to receive the English papers from Raoul's mother. Then one day, without either warning or explanation, the Mystic forbade me to go to the village to fetch them, saying, "In future no papers are to be brought into the abbey, nor must any of the members read them. Disobedience will entail banishment from the abbey."

Needless to say, I did not submit to his decree, but fetched my papers as usual, and retired after lunch to read them in my own room. I had not been reading long when the Mystic strode in, his face twitching with rage. He ordered me to go. There was a terrific scene. I should have said before that there were several loaded revolvers which used to lie about in the abbey. They were very necessary, for we never knew whether brigands might not attack it. The Mystic used to shoot any dogs that came anywhere near the abbey with his revolver. He was an extremely good shot. It so happened that I had found one of these revolvers lying about the day before, and it suddenly occurred to me that it would be a wise precaution to hide it under my pillow. I now seized it and fired it wildly at the Mystic. It went wide of the mark. He laughed heartily. Then I rushed at him, but could not get a grip on his shaved head. He picked me up in his arms and flung me bodily outside, through the front door.

I was well aware how it would distress Raoul and endanger his slender chances of recovery to be parted from me at this time. And yet I knew that no amount of persuasion would induce the Mystic to allow me to return. I therefore determined to write to the British consul at Palermo and appeal for his assistance.

I found temporary accommodation in the village, and at once proceeded with my design. However, while I was still engaged in writing I was intruded upon by one of the women of the abbey, who saw what I was doing before I had time to take any measures of concealment, and immediately reported it to the Mystic, who from what followed must, I think, have been somewhat perturbed by my intention. For the next day this same woman brought me a note from Raoul begging me to return even if I had to climb through the window. I went straight to the abbey, where the Mystic greeted me with the ultimatum that I must sign a paper denying the statements about the abbey that I had made in my letter to the consul. For Raoul's sake I complied and was allowed to remain.

The next morning Raoul was much worse. The Mystic was visibly alarmed and sent an urgent summons to the doctor. On seeing Raoul, the doctor at once dispatched me to the village for some special oil which was to be injected by means of a hypodermic syringe. I made all the haste I could, and as a result of my exertion combined with a natural anxiety, fainted in the shop. When I came to I saw the Mystic standing over me. He said kindly, "There, that's better. You're all right now."

There was a cab waiting outside in which we drove as far towards the abbey as the track allowed, continuing our journey on foot. It was late in the afternoon, and the setting sun touched the arid rock-strewn hillside with pink. Then suddenly, just as the sun was about to disappear beneath the horizon, the Mystic stopped, and said,

"We will take adoration" (a daily rite in the abbey), and raising his hand he pronounced the customary and to me then beautiful invocation. Before he had finished I observed that tears were running down his cheeks, and for his sympathy and love for Raoul I forgave him everything.

The invocation done, we went on our way. But before we had gone far a woman from the abbey met us. She was distressed.

"Is he worse?" I asked fearfully.

"He's dead," she answered. I fainted again.

When I came to I was led into the room where my husband had died. He lay there on the bed, his arms raised slightly behind the head, while the head was drooping forward slightly, in exactly the same position as the spirit form on the photograph that had been taken on our wedding day. It had been a warning.

In Italy a corpse may not remain in the house after sunset. Raoul's body was placed in a coffin, which was then carried to a sort of greenhouse at the side of the abbey. The coffin lid was removed, and Raoul lay inside looking just as if he were asleep. All night long the Mystic in his robes paced round the coffin, tapping it with his wand and muttering incantations. I shall never forget that tapping. For months it echoed in my head. At last morning came. Raoul could not be buried actually inside the cemetery as he was not a Catholic, but a piece of ground was got outside just by the road, along the hillside. I did not join the service, which was conducted by the Mystic clad in his most magnificent vestments, with precious stones gleaming on his hands, with the women of the abbey round him, weeping. I watched from a little distance off. I have never seen such crowds as those that came to poor Raoul's burial. From miles round peasants came in, for the abbey was known all over Sicily. The sun made the white domes of the sepulchres sparkle. Away below the cliff the sea dashed itself on the stones. The Mystic stood with his

magic wand raised. It was at least such a burial as
Raoul himself would have wished for.

Three days later money arrived through the consul,
and I left for England.

CHAPTER VIII

I GO TO AMERICA

Jacob Kramer—A fox-hunting painter—A mad visit to
Yorkshire—Poverty—I appear in the papers—Princess
Waletka—New York—Broadway—An Indian Reservation—
Montreal—I part with Waletka—I return home—I meet
Carol—Marriage again—Life in the country—My shop—The
Rookery—Carol's illness—I run away.

On my return to London I put up at the Harlequin Club,
in the room I had shared with Raoul during the early days
of our marriage. At first I felt very lonely and depressed,
but my spirits gradually improved and my melancholy
recollections were pushed into the background by a
chance meeting with an old friend—the Jewish painter,
Jacob Kramer—whom I had not seen or communicated
with for years.

The feeling of returning to London after a long
absence is one which I find never palls on me. As soon
as my train approaches whichever terminus it happens
to be, and I see out of the window the familiar backs
of the tenement houses, with their washing and their
outside staircases, my memories of wherever I have been
staying, of the people I have met and the things I have
done suddenly seem very remote, and I am possessed
with an incredible eagerness to resume all the activities

and to visit all the places that I have neglected for so long. Directly I get out on to the platform I call a taxi and drive to the Fitzroy Tavern in Charlotte Street, or to wherever I think I am likely to find some of my friends. So I acted on this occasion. I should add, by the way, that there is nowhere quite like the Fitzroy. It seems more of a café than a public house, or at least as like a café as anything I know in England. Its proprietor, Mr. Kleinfeld, and his very charming daughter Annie, are some of the nicest and kindest people I know, and I am sure there are lots of people like me who feel they could not do without them. It was here that I met Jacob. He has now become quite famous in his profession. In those days, however, he was as yet little known, and in consequence hard up. It is a source of no little satisfaction to me that his present reputation is due in some part to myself, since a portrait he did of me called "The Sphinx" was exhibited among the modern pictures that were shown at the Wembley Exhibition, and was greatly admired.

This was done for a manufacturer of Bradford, who met me in the Harlequin, and was so taken with my appearance and personality that he commissioned Jacob to paint me for quite a large sum. He also, very generously, paid me for my sittings.

The work was done in my room at the Harlequin, as Jacob was then too poor to afford a studio, and while painting the picture quickly fell in love with me. It was here he proposed to me, and we arranged to get married as soon as the picture was finished and the fee paid. His mother, however, as a practising Jew, refused to allow him to marry a Christian.

But, after all, I wonder whether perhaps this was just as well, for I do not think Jacob was designed for a solid and easy-going husband. As soon as he got the money he gave a series of parties at The Yorkshire Grey in Fitzroy Street, which was then the meeting-place of a considerable artistic circle. Here I met a remarkable man, Brooks, the fox-hunting painter, and his wife Pete, who was once one of Epstein's most promising pupils, but has done little serious sculpture since her marriage.

About this time my life began to become rather incoherent, and I will tell you the following incident to show the sort of thing I mean.

One day someone casually suggested that we should all go to Yorkshire. Everybody immediately fell in with the idea and we set off on the spot, arriving late at Grassington the same night.

We remained at Grassington until someone else had another whim. This time to go to Leeds to visit some friends and patrons of art called S——. They wanted me to accompany them, but I preferred to remain where I was staying. About a fortnight later, however, we decided to follow our friends.

We had arranged to catch the eleven o'clock train, and arrived at the station with some ten minutes to spare. But our precaution failed in its effect. To fill in the time, it was suggested that we should have a drink at the pub opposite the station, and there, incredible as it may sound, we remained until five o'clock in the afternoon. One member of the party alleges that I beat him at billiards.

At five o'clock we sent another wire and caught a train to Leeds. We all fell asleep *en route*. Someone met us at the station, and we all adjourned to the station bar for another drink to pull us together and prepare us for an encounter with the S——s. Then just as we were leaving the station another of the party announced his intention of going to London. His wife accompanied him, and the rest of us went to the S——s's house alone.

We found there Bob S—— (a medical student at Leeds University), Olive his wife (once a model of Augustus John's. Now a wealthy woman, owing to a previous husband who had died only a fortnight after the marriage), and, to my delight, my old friend Ralph, with whom I had been through some hard times soon after the war. He was apparently living in rooms in Leeds and having his meals with the S——s. Olive, since acquiring her money, was an extremely generous benefactress to poor artists, and she had bought a number of pictures both by Ralph and other friends of mine.

Although it was rather late we had some tea, and afterwards played the guitar and sang a little, until it was time to go out to the S——s's habitual tavern for an aperitif. Here I could see that Ralph's old inclination towards me was beginning to revive. I found that I had a good deal to say to him, and after a bit I realized that we had been quite unconsciously ignoring the others. One of them, whom I will call X., was very annoyed. As soon as I turned round he said,

BETTY MAY AT THE FITZROY TAVERN. FROM A DRAWING
BY NINA HAMNETT

"I'd better go and find you a room."

"Oh, no," said Olive. "You needn't bother. Betty can stay with us."

At this X. came up to me, fuming, and began to expostulate, but I pushed him off and whispered to Olive, "For God's sake keep him away."

She understood, and from that time forward X. was not admitted to their house.

"What about some food?" Bob S—— suggested.

We agreed with his suggestion and went out, leaving X. alone and furious.

I took up my abode with the S——s, and saw Ralph every day at meals. We rapidly got fond of one another again and took to going for walks together in the afternoons, and he asked me to sit for him. On one of our walks we met X. He came up and attempted to join us, but we took no notice of him, and at length, after making some unwarrantable assertions, he went away. That, we thought, was the last of him. But we were wrong.

One afternoon we had all been out for a motor drive, and Bob and Ralph were garaging the car while Olive and I went on home. When we turned into our street the first thing we saw was X., mad-drunk, with dishevelled hair, attacking the S——s's front door with a hatchet. We were terrified. I thought our best plan was to slip in by the back entrance and telephone for the police. Telephoning, however, proved unnecessary, as the police had already arrived. In fact we met them in the hall—with X.

The inspector was stern. Having ascertained Olive's credentials, he turned to me.

"Are you anything to do with this man?" he asked, indicating X.

"I *was*," I replied, thinking impudence to be the best policy.

"Oh, you were," said the inspector sagely, "were you?"

I nodded.

"Well," he went on, "will you see that he leaves Leeds before twelve o'clock to-night? Otherwise I shall have to lock him up."

I agreed that I would.

X. was recalcitrant and refused to go unless I promised to accompany him, which I was at length compelled to do. He would probably have been even less amenable had he known that I had bought a return ticket for myself. When we got to London I gave X. the slip while he was buying a paper and returned straight to Leeds, where Ralph was awaiting me on the platform.

In course of time Ralph became bored with Leeds and had an idea that he would like to do some landscapes, and asked if we would accompany him.

We went to a delightful village called Horton, near Ribblesdale, where we found an equally pleasant inn to put up at. Every day we used to go out painting, taking our lunch with us, and in the evening we conversed with the rustics over ale. I was very happy. But after about three months I began to long for London. Ralph asked me why I wanted to go.

"Oh, I'm just fed up," I said.

"With us?"

"No. With the country. I feel I must go back to London. That's all."

Somewhat reluctantly they allowed me to go. And so I found myself back in London once more.

I now found myself in very low water. For some reason there seemed to be very little opportunity for getting sittings, and I could not get a job anywhere dancing or anything like that.

I was miserably poor. I lived in a tiny attic in Soho, for which I paid twelve shillings and sixpence a week. I had only one dress, which I used to wash myself and put on wet. Often I had nothing to eat all day. I was pretty well finished when a press photographer called and asked me to give him a sitting. Here at last, I thought, was a possibility of making a guinea or so. But the event exceeded my hopes. For one evening while I was sitting in the "Plough," near the British Museum, I was introduced to a journalist who suggested that my life-story would be of interest to his paper. We talked together for a long time, and I told him all about some of the exciting portions of my life in Limehouse and Paris and Sicily. He was very interested in the story. I told him that if he wanted to get hold of me he had better ring up the "Crown" in Brewer Street between six and seven. The proprietors of the "Crown" were, at this time, Mr. and Mrs. Morris and their daughter, all of whom were very kind to me at this period when I was poor. I shall always be very grateful to them for this. I don't forget that sort of thing.

BETTY MAY. FROM A DRAWING BY GERALD REITLINGER

Three weeks later he rang up and asked me to dine with him, adding that he had some good news for me. I went to the meeting-place in a state of great excitement. He was waiting for me.

"Oh," I exclaimed, without any other greeting, "what is the news? Tell me quickly."

He had not deluded me. The news was that a Sunday paper had offered to pay £500 for some articles describing some of my adventures.

I was thrilled. The publicity! To see my name in the headlines every week! To impress my personality on the public—and they would be impressed, I felt sure, for no one has had such a life as mine. And then there was the money. I could hardly restrain myself from shouting aloud and throwing my arms around his neck there and then.

"How too marvellous!" I said. "Bernard, you are a dear."

And so it was settled.

"Now," I announced, "we must celebrate. I want a wonderful dinner. Let's go to the Café Royal."

I had not been there for months, and I was welcomed by the waiters as I had been long ago on my return from Paris. Bernard was infected with my excitement. We drank good luck to the life-story in large quantities of the best champagne, and after that we had some of the choicest brandy the Café Royal could produce.

I removed from my Soho lodging, and took a nice flat. Here I led a very tolerable life. Every day I used to go down to lunch in Fleet Street, where I got to know a number of the leading journalists. In Bernard's own office I was a great favourite from the beginning, and I increased my popularity by making tea for the staff in the afternoon.

One day on Bernard's table I saw a photograph of a remarkable looking woman, and from that moment determined to make her acquaintance. I asked Bernard who she was, but could only get out of him that she was a clairvoyant of sorts, about whom he was writing an article, and when I requested him to take me to see her, he replied vaguely that she was very difficult to approach. I was not to be put off, however.

"I desire to meet her," I said. "And what is more, I will meet her. Will you take me?"

He rather unwillingly consented, probably believing that I should forget all about her in a few days' time. But he was wrong. I had definitely made up my mind that I was going to meet her and refused to be satisfied until I had done so. I pestered him daily until at last he announced that he had persuaded her to come to tea at the Waldorf Hotel.

I almost trembled with excitement as we awaited her arrival. I felt that the meeting would be somehow momentous, that it would vitally affect my life. I kept my eyes fixed on the revolving doors through which we had come in, but everyone went straight to a table. None paused to look round in search of us. At last Bernard stood up and gesticulated to someone who had entered by another door. I eagerly looked in the same direction, and saw approaching us a gaunt, swarthy woman of Red Indian type, with large intense eyes, long plaits of black hair and moccasins. With her was a little boy of about seven, and her husband.

Without being introduced, she said to me,

"You are Betty May. You have been married three times and your last husband, who was younger than you, died of fever. Is not that so?" She spoke slowly in a deep voice, with a peculiar rhythmic intonation that was both impressive and compelling.

"You are a twin soul of mine," she went on, without waiting for an answer to her question. "Our destinies are interwoven. When I die you will die too."

All this time her deep hypnotic eyes stared into mine, and I felt as if all my personality, every scrap of vitality, was being drawn out of me by that gaze. If she moved, I moved. For the time being at any rate, I was not even a twin soul. I was the same soul. My centre was in her.

"You will come with me to America," she said, and I knew that I could not do otherwise.

The next day I left the flat and went to live in the household of this strange woman, who was known as the Princess Waletka.

Not long after I joined her we set out on a provincial tour. Waletka was everywhere successful, as indeed she deserved to be, since her thought-reading methods baffled even Houdini. However, when we were in a certain important town in South Wales, her popularity was the cause of an incident which reminded me that the publicity derived from the weekly instalments of my life-story (they had now been running for some time) was not without its disadvantages. Some very rich people who were well known in the neighbourhood gave a luncheon in Waletka's honour, which I also attended. We had just sat down and started our *hors-d'oeuvres* when our hostess asked me, " Your name is Betty May, isn't it ? "

" Yes," I answered.

" May I ask," she went on, "if you are the Betty May whose life has been appearing in the —— ? "

Again I replied that I was indeed.

" In that case," she said, "I must ask you to leave my house immediately."

Amazed, I rose from my place and went out. Waletka followed me, saying, "If my friend goes, I go."

Not long after this we sailed to America.

How shall I give my impressions of America ?

I hardly know. The absolutely equal vividness of my experiences, and the rapidity with which they succeeded one another, prevented me from retaining any distinct or orderly recollections of them. I was in America for three months. But I find it impossible to say, "This happened at such and such a time, and that just before, and that just after." Those three months dwell in my mind as one single, though composite experience. I remember them as one remembers a particular evening, after a certain interval has elapsed. Let me, however, try to disentangle some of the more important facts about that memory.

The first is the overwhelming hospitality of the Americans. We stayed most of the time in New York, and were never away for more than a few days together. Nevertheless we always had more offers of entertainment than we could possibly avail ourselves of.

I had an opportunity of seeing something of American home life, which is so different from ours, when I stayed with the charming Mr. and Mrs. Morris in their country house. As you know, he is probably the biggest theatrical producer in America, and he and his wife were extremely kind to us.

Our acquaintance was very largely theatrical. Indeed the atmosphere of the theatre pervades my entire recollection of America. One of the things that I do remember very vividly is Broadway. What a wonderful street it is when lighted up at night. Even all I had heard and read about it did not prepare me for what it was really like. Nearly every night Waletka gave a performance either in New York or its environs, and as I try now to picture myself at that time I seem to see a succession of dressing-rooms, all of them bare, dusty, draughty and smelling of grease-paint. All furnished with the same mirrors and hand-basins (the water usually cold) and make-up tables. All of them littered with costumes and properties which, it seemed to me, could never be got back again into their trunks. Soon I felt at home in any dressing-room. I became used to sitting there with Waletka's little boy, Neil, all the time his mother was on the stage. I knew every cue by heart and at any point could tell to a second how much longer the performance was going on for. In a week I felt as if I had been connected with the stage all my life.

After the theatre we often went to the most sumptuous supper parties. And if we had a few days free of engagements we used to go for delightful automobile trips to Saranac Lake or the Adirondack Hills. There is a sanatorium for consumptives at Saranac, the air being considered particularly beneficial to people so afflicted, on account of the abundance of pine trees. This, I think, was the reason why we went there so often, for both Waletka and her daughter suffered from consumption.

There was a mayoral election in progress during my visit, and Waletka and many of the theatrical celebrities of New York combined to give a charity concert on behalf of the republican candidate. The place chosen for the performance was a little town called Glens Falls, on the Canadian border, where intoxicating liquor could be bought and consumed—though only after complying with a multitude of vexatious and pointless formalities. After the concert a public banquet was provided for the performers, at which I had my first drink since landing in America. And how I appreciated it! Everybody around me seemed also to be taking advantage of the greater indulgence of the British law, and in no half-hearted fashion. I felt almost as if I were at home again, at a party in the Café Royal. I was in my element. I would show these people how to revel. For good drinkers as they were, they had not known such parties as I had, in the old days of Billie Carleton. They had not known the Crabtree and the Cabaret Club and the Endell Street Club! My mind went back to my earliest times in London, to the wonderful pre-war London, in comparison with which the present seems so insipid. I wondered vaguely if I should ever go back, or if I should spend the rest of my life here in America.

My reverie was interrupted by a chorus of voices shouting my name. It was my turn to entertain the company with a song. I sang "The Raggle-Taggle Gipsies"—one of the songs I used to sing to Epstein while he was modelling his bust of me—and it was received with demonstrations of enthusiastic appreciation.

Strongly contrasted with the gay parties at Glens Falls was my visit to the Indian reservation of Coughnawaga. Here we found a way of life grave, primitive, monotonous—the absolute opposite to the restless "go-getting" of Wall Street and Fifth Avenue. We were the guests of the chief, and stayed in his hut. He was, by the way, the father of the chief figure in the famous Stillman case of a few years ago. He showed us a number of interesting things, including the Indian method of making bread and "Pemmican," pounded in a way of which they only know the secret. It is useful for long expeditions, when the weight and bulk of food carried has to be reduced to a minimum. He also showed us the "huskies," or wolf-crossed sleigh dogs, that snarled and snapped from their cages all day long. His wife, too, was very kind to us. As a matter of fact the Indians rather disappointed me, as they wore quite ordinary European clothes, and as a result looked rather uninteresting and not at all picturesque.

From here we went to Montreal, a beautiful town, and a great contrast to New York. For Montreal retains the tranquillity which I believe, though I have never visited them, still characterizes the towns of the old slave-owning states of the South. At any rate I found it restful after the gaiety and clatter of Broadway.

I think now that my homesickness really began in Montreal, though I was not conscious of it at the time. We returned to New York to fulfil a number of engagements, both social and professional, and I took part in them with an apparently undiminished zest. But I can see now that my energy was flagging. I was indulging in a feverish activity to disguise my dissatisfaction from myself, and to repress any timid homesickness that had I stopped to reflect might make itself heard. One day, however, among the Adirondack Hills, my sleeping desire to see England again awakened, and would not be put off or evaded, and I said to Waletka,

"I must go home."

She was sorry, because of her affection for me, and because she had hoped that I might, with training, have been able to assist her in her profession, but with true insight she made no effort to dissuade me from my intention. And so I went back to New York for the last time. Waletka bought me some beautiful dresses as a parting present. She paid my fare and gave me a hundred pounds. She came on board the ship with me so as to postpone saying good-bye until the last possible moment. I remember how moved she was, but little else of the journey, as my thoughts were already directed towards England.

I then took up my life again at the point where I had broken it off to go to America.

Three days after landing in England I happened to go into the "Crown "in Brewer Street, where I met my old friend Jacob. He was delighted to see me, and we spent a very talkative five minutes relating what each of us had been doing in the time that had passed since last we met. Then Jacob said he must go, as he had an appointment. (It is a peculiarity of Jacob's that he has more appointments per day than any man I know.) "I won't be long," he said. "I'm just going to meet a man. I'll try and bring him back here. Will you wait?"

About half an hour later he returned with a youth whom he introduced to me as Carol, the assistant editor of a well-known sporting paper. Carol was a positive, assertive sort of person, not to say opinionated, as he showed by his first remark to me, "I wish you'd take some of the rouge off your lips. I think it looks horrible. And I detest polished nails."

Nevertheless, before closing time he had given me as a present a national flag of Wales, and obtained permission to ring me up.

A few days later the telephone bell rang in our flat, and when I answered it an unfamiliar voice asked, "Is that Miss Betty May?"

"Yes," I replied. "Who's that?"

"Carol," the voice said. I have a bad memory for names and inquired who he was, anyway.

"I gave you a Welsh flag a few days ago," he said. "Will you dine with me to-night?"

I accepted his invitation and turned up wearing the

flag as a headdress, a delicate compliment, I thought, to the donor. Carol, however, was not pleased. He was as particular, I discovered, about women's attire as Raoul had been about his own. A woman, in his eyes, must above all things be correctly dressed, or, as he used to express it, "Well turned out." Nevertheless, we continued to lunch and dine together almost every day.

You will by now probably have guessed where this was going to lead. And if you have done so you have also probably guessed right. After a short time it was agreed that we should get married. I suppose that in a way it was silly of me to agree to it, but, after all, you cannot really help falling in love when it comes to the point. Carol liked hunting and shooting and fishing, and I do not really care for that sort of thing, as I have already tried to explain. I knew it would mean living in the country again, but the days when I had done this before seemed so far off that I had almost forgotten how much I had disliked it. And, anyway, I do not think about that sort of thing much when I suddenly find that I am fond of someone. So we got engaged and once more I began making arrangements and plans for another marriage.

Carol, meanwhile, had acquainted his mother with his intention of getting married. She was not pleased. And her misgivings were increased by frequent calls of condolence from the neighbours, among whom Carol had spread the rumour that I was a fat negress with five children.

I left my flat immediately and moved into a room procured for me by Carol. The landlady was an Italian and a very pleasant woman. But after a while she raised a very curious objection. Carol had given her to understand that I was his wife. He was in the habit of leaving notes for me, if by any chance I was out in the middle of the day when he called. The landlady one day, to my great surprise, asked for my rent and said she could no longer have me in her house, on the ground that husbands did not as a rule continually leave notes for their wives! "But," she added, "I am sure my sister would be very glad to have you."

If was at the sister's house that the first great scene with my mother-in-law took place.

Soon after it had become understood that we were to be married, Carol thought it would be advisable for me to meet his mother and make as good an impression on her as I could. We also decided, in view of his mother's character, that it would be advisable to pretend that we were already married, and so to compel her to acknowledge as a fact what she would never have consented to. We accordingly went down to the country the following week-end.

Carol's mother was one of those cold, drooping ladies who seem to live more because "one must" than for any other reason. Her only hold on life was her fierce love for her son, which appeared almost a mania. She was obviously hostile to myself from the start, though I must say she was too much of a lady not to try her level best to hide from me what she felt. I supposed I was one of the things that "did happen."

It was not a comfortable week-end. Poor Carol—I

felt very sorry for him—tried rather uneasily to get some understanding between his mother and myself, but for all his efforts he was unable to find a single topic of conversation interesting to us both. In the end he gave up the attempt and confined himself to talking now to one and now to the other, on subjects, and even in a language, which were of their nature absolutely unintelligible to the third person. When his mother and I were alone she kept up the conventions by telling me about her relations.

On Monday morning when the maid awakened me with my tea, I murmured to myself with heart-felt sincerity, "Well, thank goodness that's over." The ordeal was over, and, I flattered myself, not too disastrously. Our visit might have been put down even as a great success had it not been for Carol. I cannot think what possessed him to say it, and can only think that it was the same impish humour that made him spread the rumour that I was a black woman. At all events, and whatever the explanation, he said casually to his mother just as we were getting into the car to go to the station,

"Oh, by the way, mother, we aren't married, of course."

Her reaction to this news may be guessed.

Carol and I went to a party that night and did not arrive home until some time after three o'clock a.m. At six the landlady came in and told us that a lady had been to the house the previous afternoon, inquiring for me.

"What a good thing I was out," I said.

"She said she was coming back early this morning," the landlady added.

We had a terrible scene when she did arrive. Carol was also there by that time. She abused me and entreated me. She called me a wicked woman. She wept and begged me on her knees to give her back her son. It was impossible to stop her, and Carol and I looked on helplessly. Every now and then he touched her shoulder and said nervously, "Mother, do stop."

At length she could continue no longer. She dabbed her eyes and nose and rearranged her hat in front of the mirror.

"You will get married, won't you?" she gasped as she departed, buttoning her gloves.

After the wedding Carol took me down to his home, where it was decided we should live for the time being. We arrived in time for tea, which his mother poured out, remarking to me as she did so,

"I'm not sure that you oughtn't to be pouring out instead of me now."

When we had finished Carol said he must go and have a look at a part of the river he was baiting for the week-end. I immediately offered to accompany him. To get to the river we had to cross several fields, in the corner of one of which was a large rookery. Carol looked up, as we passed, at the birds, and said,

"I really must come out one day and shoot some of them. There are far too many. I've been meaning to for a long time. But what with getting married and one thing and another . . ."

At this moment I stepped into a concealed rut and fell

over, twisting my ankle slightly and losing, as on another previous occasion, one of my shoes.

Carol picked me up and asked if I had hurt myself.

"No," I replied, "but my feet are horribly wet, and I've ruined this coat."

"Yes," he agreed, "you are in a bit of a mess."

And added, as an afterthought, "By the way, you'll have to get some rather more suitable kit for shooting and so forth."

We met a lot of farmers and yokels on the way. Carol knew them all and asked nearly every one of them some such question as, "Have you seen any more of that covey we put up on so-and-so's the other day?" or "Has old so-and-so lost any more chickens?"

The fish were apparently satisfactory, since Carol merely looked at the water and did nothing further about them. Personally I thought the whole expedition seemed a little pointless.

On the way home we went into the "Bull," the chief public house of the village, and about a mile from our house, for a drink. Carol introduced me to the landlord, who was very amused at my not being black, and frankly doubtful about my reputed five children. However, having expressed his views he had nothing further to say to me, and proceeded to the more important business of informing Carol of the sporting and agricultural news of the neighbourhood.

"Will you be in here to-night?" he asked Carol as we were leaving. "I expect Mr. —— will look in."

"Yes," said Carol, "I want to see him."

Carol was, by profession, a sporting journalist, and he used to visit the "Bull," as this tavern was called, in order to find out if any surprising fish had been caught, what the prospects of the pheasant season were, or what the recent bags of partridges had been, and so forth. The "Bull" was the home of all the sporting as well as agricultural and purely personal news of the neighbourhood, and it was on this account he had to spend his evenings there. Nevertheless, his absence was no less irksome to me than if it had been pleasure, not duty, that called him away. For the result was that I had to spend the time between dinner and bed in the sole company of his mother, with whom, for all her excellent qualities, I was unable to converse with any ease. So strained were our relations that I was very soon driven to jigsaw puzzles as the only means of filling in a decent interval before retiring for the night. The knowledge that we were now legally mother and daughter did not seem to have brought Carol's mother and myself any nearer together. It was distressing but true. However, I do not think that either of us realized at the time the true horror of it. As even if we admitted to ourselves that there could never be any sympathy between us, even if our hope be taken away, even so we neither of us had the slightest idea on that evening of the nerve-strain, the silence and hate that were to envelop us during the winter evenings that were to come.

After dinner Carol went out. We went into the drawing-room. She took some sewing from a work-basket. The maid brought in coffee.

"Do you like a lot of sugar?" she inquired as the maid was going out.

After the door shut we relapsed again into silence.

I could hear her breathing.

At length she felt that it was her duty to say something. Folding up her needlework, she addressed herself to me on the only topic the least interesting to us both—Carol. She told me what a good son he had always been to her— though there *had* been trying periods. She recounted stories of his infantile pranks. She even told me, in an expansion of confidence and a lowered voice, of his first love-affair. From the love-affair we passed to her habitual standby, or conversational stockpot, as it were—the family. Oh, those relations of hers! They haunted me like goblins. I knew all their faces even better than I knew those of my husband and my mother-in-law herself. The whole house was inhabited by them. Gradually I got by heart every detail of their dreary lives. After I had been a month married, I could have got 100 per cent. in an examination on the family history, including every younger branch, to the third and fourth generations at least.

I said I was so tired as a result of my journey that I got to bed at last by the time Carol returned from the "Bull." The next morning he went, as usual, to London, only returning in time for dinner, and going out again to the "Bull" afterwards.

On Saturdays he remained at home, and if it were the right season I would accompany him on shooting or fishing expeditions, in neither of which could I bring myself to take a great deal of interest, although he instructed me diligently in the theory and practice of both.

On Sundays we attended church, and ate a heavier lunch than on week-days.

As time went on my mother-in-law began to forget her hostility. She got accustomed to seeing me about, and liked, I suppose, the presence of someone on whom to unload her thoughts. At any rate, whatever the reason, she grew more persistent in her companionship, even following me to my bed (whither I used to retire each night at nine o'clock with a novel), and there repeating and going over all she had said during the day.

This affability, however, had, I am afraid, no softening effect upon my disposition towards her. It repulsed rather than attracted me, and further added to the touchy condition of my nerves. A climax was inevitable. This is how it happened. I had stayed in bed for breakfast as I felt slightly unwell, asking Carol to have a pot of tea and some toast sent up to me. Instead of the maid, my mother-in-law herself (very kindly) brought me what I had asked for. Unfortunately I was not in a mood to appreciate her good intentions. Couldn't she, I asked myself, even let me be ill in peace?

"Here's your breakfast, dear," she said, to call my attention from the Edgar Wallace I was engaged on.

"Thanks," I said rudely, without looking up.

But she did not take the hint.

"How are you feeling, dear?" she inquired with exasperating forbearance.

"Awful!"

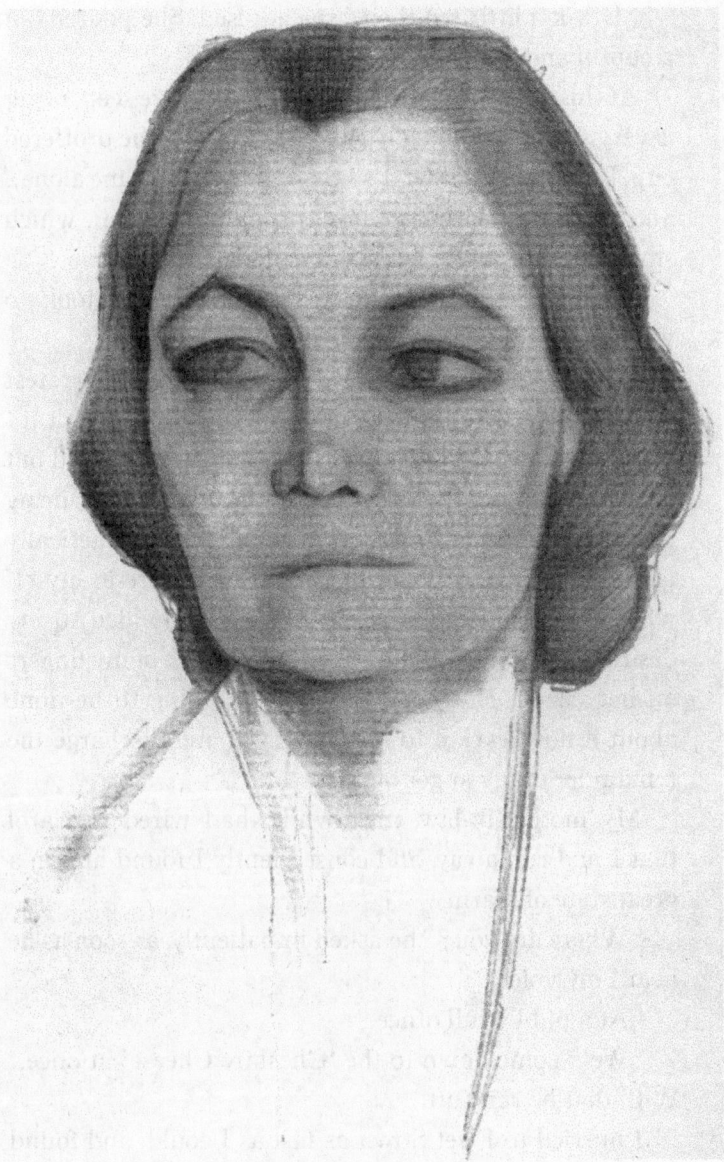

BETTY MAY. FROM A DRAWING BY MICHAEL SEVIER

"Drink a little tea then," she advised. She poured out a cupful and handed it to me.

At this my self-control, which, as you have seen, never is very strong, completely gave way. Seizing the proffered cup, I shouted: "For God's sake, woman, leave me alone," and flung the tea in her face, dropping the cup, which smashed into small pieces on the floor.

"Oh, my beautiful cup!" she wailed, and took to weeping.

I was in such a state that it was with the greatest difficulty that I refrained from slapping her face. I leapt out of bed, and in spite of my illness, dressed, rushed out of the house, and took the first train to London. During the whole journey I was so angry as to be practically unable to think. All I could do was to picture to myself what she would have looked like had I yielded to my desire to assault her. I almost felt the smack of my fingers on her cheek. However, there was nothing to be done about it now, except to ring up Carol and discharge the remainder of my anger on him.

My mother-in-law, meanwhile, had wired to Carol that I had run away, and consequently I found him in a great state of alarm.

"Where are you?" he asked impatiently, as soon as he heard my voice.

"At a public call office."

"Well, come down to the 'Cheshire Cheese' at once." With that he rang off.

I hurried to Fleet Street as fast as I could, and found him awaiting me. Before I could step inside the bar he jumped up, caught me by my arm, and dragged me away with such force that he sent an American girl reeling from the threshold of Dr. Johnson's dining-room into a waiter with a tray full of empty tankards, upsetting the lot. He had a taxi waiting outside, into which I was bundled. The driver was directed to take us to Paddington.

Carol was extremely agitated.

"As you can't be trusted to stay at home while I'm away," he announced, "I shall give up going to London. I resigned my job in the office directly I got mother's wire."

He kept his promise. From that day forward he never left the village, and hardly ever the house, without me. In some ways this made life more tolerable, for I still liked him. But it entailed the disadvantage of a much heavier programme of sport. Every day now, bar Sundays, instead of, as before, Saturdays only, was devoted to this. Even the close seasons brought little relief, as there were always rabbits and rooks.

The situation between my mother-in-law and myself was temporarily eased by the recent storm, but it was safe to guess that if the same sort of thing happened again I should probably behave in the same way. It was with the idea of preventing such a scene happening again that an arrangement was made whereby Carol and I should furnish and live quite independently in a bungalow adjoining the house. Carol most fortunately came by some money at about this time, which I spent lavishly on curtains, carpets, chair covers, rugs, lampshades, table cloths and other household articles, both useful and decorative. I enjoyed myself enormously and purchased with zest. And when the buying was done I worked like a Trojan, sewing curtains, experimenting with different arrangements of furniture, and even whitewashing and distempering. At length I had prepared as trim a little love-nest as can be imagined. It only remained for us to live there.

At first everything went as smoothly as a honeymoon. I enjoyed being able to cook once more, and made Carol such exquisite little dinners as I had once made for Raoul. He was very appreciative of my efforts. Sometimes we would collaborate in the invention of new dishes.

But alas! The pleasures of housekeeping grew stale as fast as the other pleasures of this provoking world. After about a fortnight of Darby-and-Joan in the bungalow I fled back to the house, eager to taste a meal that I had not supervised at every stage.

And after another fortnight of conversation about the family history I fled as quickly back to the bungalow. And so on.

Then I hit upon what seemed to me an admirable plan for avoiding both the family history and excessive sport. We possessed a large tent in which we were accustomed to spend a certain portion of each summer if the weather permitted. I erected this and fitted it out as a cake and sweet shop, which I ran single-handed, even to the making of all the confections sold in it. It was hard work. But in spite of my previously confessed lack of business qualities, I made a success of it. As in my dressing and in my ordinary cooking, I had no great respect for tradition or convention, and my recipes were things I invented myself, and not things I had read about.

Every day I would make some new experiment. At first the neighbourhood was a little distrustful of my wares. Gradually, however, and a little self-consciously—they felt it was odd that Carol's wife should engage in retail trade—they took to patronizing my shop, and once they had overcome their caution and their shyness they invariably became regular customers. "Miss Betty's" cakes and sweets were the admiration of the village.

Only at home my shop was disregarded, and practically never mentioned. Carol, satisfied that I had not run away, was completely taken up with his own pursuits (he still wrote a good many sporting articles and was a correspondent for the district to several papers). My mother-in-law, though she had not openly protested, had disapproved from the first. Nevertheless, I persevered, glad in some ways to have a sphere in which I was entirely independent. But in time, as with the bungalow, the drudgery became more noticeable than the pleasure. To get up on a cold morning, when it mattered to nobody except myself whether I stayed in bed or not, seemed rather pointless. If only Carol had shown the slightest interest, if he had casually said, "I think your shop's an excellent thing, Betty, I should keep on with it," I should have gladly taken his advice. But as his attitude—I forget the exact words—was one of "Please yourself," I stayed in bed, gave up the shop, and was more bored than ever.

By way of amusing myself, I returned for the third time to the bungalow. But I found it no more satisfactory than on previous occasions. I felt as if we were playing at independence, like children. And when, as soon happened, the game grew tedious, there was nothing left for me but surrender.

In the following of this new policy I listened with close attention to my husband's instructions and stories about sport, and tried to put them into practice, if not with much success, at least with a good deal of enthusiasm.

One afternoon Carol said, "The rookery is really getting hopelessly over-populated. I think we'll go and shoot some to-day. I've been meaning to for a long time."

"Ever since I came here."

"Oh, no, much longer than that."

He went to fetch his gun. I felt a little depressed. Could I keep this up for ever? I wondered. Could I be content to give up my own life, without even the reward of being assured that my sacrifice was appreciated? Could I adapt myself absolutely to his ways, if he made no effort to respond to my desire to be loved and to be told so? It seemed a long time since that first walk when he had mentioned the rooks to me, but the reaches of time before us seemed even longer.

Carol returned, wiping the oil from his rifle with a rag.

"Have you got the sandwiches?" he asked.

We set out. It was a wonderful autumn morning. The rookery was in a thin belt of trees on the top of a ridge, and the sun, which rose from the earth, glowed through the mist.

Carol, in a brown shooting coat and a tweed hat stuck with trout flies, a cigarette in his mouth and his gun under his arm, looked utterly in keeping with the scene.

The noise, as we approached the wood, grew

deafening. When at length we got among the trees I felt as if I were beneath a black canopy, that creaked in the slight wind. Then Carol started to shoot. The great birds rained down. I was terrified in case one should fall on me. They flapped about our feet. Carol instructed me to break the necks of those that still struggled. I can hardly describe the repulsion that I felt at the idea of touching them. Nevertheless, I did as he said, though it nearly made me sick. For hours I was engaged on this disgusting task. Dusk fell while I was still doing it.

We gathered our spoil and walked heavily home. I felt tired and unhappy, and was oppressed with a sensation of foreboding. For the last three nights a screech owl had settled on our house, and the villagers all said it was an omen of death. Upon entering the home meadow we heard a cry.

A week after the slaughter of the rooks Carol was taken ill with some form of internal poisoning. The symptoms were a high temperature and continuous vomiting. I was convinced that the rook pie, which I had firmly refused to eat, was the cause.

When after several days had elapsed and he showed no signs of improvement, we began to feel extremely anxious about him. (I could not forget the screech owl.) His mother broke down completely. She did nothing beyond sitting about the house with red eyes and a swollen face, and refusing to eat. The business of nursing fell entirely upon me, and I am bound to admit that in some ways I was not ungrateful for having something to do.

Carol's illness was a serious one, and likely to be

prolonged. Our bedroom was fitted out as a sick room. We had a nurse in to be with him at night, the doctor's visits became part of our routine, and one had a feeling that the illness had already lasted a very long time.

My mother-in-law grew more nervous every day, until the doctor was almost as anxious about her as about Carol. She ate hardly anything, and never slept, often wandering about the house at all hours of the night in a dressing-gown, and creeping into the sick room, much to the irritation of the nurse, who, at length, complained to the doctor. Her behaviour towards me made things very difficult. When the doctor, on the nurse's complaint, requested her to cease her nightly visitations, and in the interests of her own health to rest if she could not sleep, she declared that he was in league with me to keep her away from her own son.

From that time onwards she took such a dislike to me that my nerves began to give way.

She always used to be present when Carol took his meals—beef-tea, bread and milk, etc., cooked by me. It so happened one morning that, immediately after consuming his breakfast, he vomited profusely. I was about to repair the misfortune when I felt my wrist seized by a cold hand.

"Oh, you foul, wicked woman," his mother accused me in a dry, throaty whisper, "you're killing my son." I felt that this was the last straw. On an earlier occasion I had refrained from attacking her with violence. This time I was too strung up to be influenced by any such scruples, and I did.

Leaving her there crying, I went straight to my own

room for my hat and coat and such luggage as I could carry. On coming out again, prepared for departure, I was horrified to see Carol at the top of the stairs in his pyjamas, holding a shot-gun.

I put down my suit-case.

Carol was swaying as if he were drunk. I dashed up to him just in time to save him from falling down the stairs. He was practically fainting. I led him back to bed.

"Now you mustn't be silly, Carol," I coaxed, stroking his forehead. "You promise you won't get out of bed while I go for the doctor."

He moved his head in assent, being incapable of speech, or so I thought until he croaked out between his gasps,

"I will, if you promise not to run away."

"Of course not, darling," I replied, although that was precisely what I intended to do.

An hour later I was once more in the train for London.

CONCLUSION

AND so now I have come to the end of my story. I suppose that at this point I should say something about the way I look at life, and give some good advice to others who may be about to embark on a similar career of adventure. Perhaps I ought to, but I certainly shall not do so. For one thing, I look upon my life as only just beginning. I am still young. I have my looks and my energy. The future holds all sorts of things in store for me, probably just as extraordinary as things that have happened to me already.

After all, when I used to wander about the East End of London as a child, it did not look as if I should get to know the underworld of Paris, sit for famous artists, be bored in English villages, watch magical rites in Sicily, or really do any of the things that have made up my life, and so I feel completely uncertain about the future.

My feeling about my life is in many ways one of great dissatisfaction. In spite of my adventures I do not really think that in many things I have got the best out of it, and yet when I look back on it I find it equally difficult to imagine myself behaving in any way differently when I remember the various problems with which I have been faced. In fact I believe enormously in the overpowering influence of Fate, which seems to haunt me equally in good or bad fortune. Against this hidden but all-powerful influence it seems to me impossible and foolish to rebel. It has brought me joy and it has brought me sadness. No doubt it will bring me both again, but I am sure that I am born for adventure, and in the future I shall be able to face these things as I have faced them in the past.

Sometimes I think I will leave England for a long period. It has crossed my mind to make my way to Africa—to Abyssinia, and again, I sometimes decide that I will go to Spain. At present I cannot make up my mind, and for once the way does not seem as clear to me as it has often done in the past. But this will not be for long. The uncertainty will not last—soon I shall decide. Perhaps I shall disappear for months—for years. But one of these days you will certainly hear of me again, and perhaps read of the further adventures of Betty May.